DA⋯ ⋯ G

TREES

DANCING
WITH
TREES

ECO-TALES FROM
THE BRITISH ISLES

ALLISON GALBRAITH
AND ALETTE J. WILLIS

*For Andy Hunter (1954–2015), our friend and a great
storyteller who brought his love for cycling and stories
together with his commitment to the environment. He was
an inspiration to all who had the good fortune to know him.*

First published 2017

The History Press
The Mill, Brimscombe Port
Stroud, Gloucestershire, gl5 2qg
www.thehistorypress.co.uk

British Library Cataloguing in Publication Data.
A catalogue record for this book is available from the British Library.

isbn 978 0 7509 7887 3

Typesetting and origination by The History Press
Printed and bound by TJ Books Ltd, Padstow, Cornwall, using environmentally
friendly paper

CONTENTS

Earth

The Web of Life

Living in Harmony

FOREWORD

Nature makes patterns and so do we. That is because we are part of nature and nature is part of us. The web of life is inclusive and interconnected.

After nearly two million years of human activity, life on planet earth has reached a crisis point. Either we humans rediscover our connectedness in all aspects of shared existence, or nature's life will go on without us. Which would be a shame since, amidst all the damage done, humanity has also made beauty, loved, and dreamed truth.

So thank God for the storytellers at this point of crisis. They understand patterns of connection and weave new understandings through their narrative web. Here are two fine examples – Allison Galbraith and Alette Willis. They live their art and their ecological awareness in mind, language, body and imagination. Here, they have produced a lovely resource of eco-tales, so that we can be part of the magic – and of the engaged, creative living that can reshape planet earth.

Read, dream and tell. The patterns are changing – new shapes are born from the old – and we can make something unexpected for the future. Stories are for pleasure, curiosity, learning and imagination. They are for everyone, together – all ages and all the families of these islands and the whole world.

Breathe fresh life into the wise old stories and let the new stories begin!

Donald Smith, August 2016
Director, TRACS (Traditional Arts and Culture Scotland)

ACKNOWLEDGEMENTS

Like all storytellers, we wish to acknowledge the generations of tellers who stand behind us, who kept these stories alive over the centuries and added their own details and nuances to them. We thank these tellers, those whom we were able to name (please see the detailed source notes at the end of the book) and those who have been lost to the tides of history. Second, we would like to thank everyone who works to bring people into more harmonious relationships with their local places and ecosystems, the planet and all that dwell here, through stories. A few of you we've had the privilege to work with, some of you we have been fortunate to meet, but most of you we don't yet know. This work of reconnection is the important work of our times. Thirdly, we'd like to thank our audiences, who have helped us hone these stories over the years. Stories are co-created between the teller and the listeners. Alette would particularly like to thank those whom she has had the joy to meet through the Talking Trees at the Royal Botanic Garden Edinburgh and the audiences who are sometimes surprised to find a storyteller at the Edinburgh Zoo. Allison would particularly like to thank all the community gardeners, foresters, countryside rangers and wildlife champions she has had the pleasure to work with and learn from over many years.

Now for the individuals to whom we owe a debt of gratitude. A big, huge thank you to Tessa Wyatt – we felt as if Christmas had come early when we saw the beautiful illustrations she had made for this book. We thank Donald Smith for his foreword and for introducing us to The History Press Folk Tales series. We thank our editor Matilda

Richards at The History Press for seeing the value in a book such as this one. Also, a special thank you to the irrepressible Mairi McFadyen for her support and encouragement along the way.

Where possible, we have drawn on multiple sources for each story retold here (again, see sources at the end of the book). However, some individuals require mentioning here. Linda Williamson needs a special thank you for advising us regarding permissions to retell stories from the estate of Duncan Williamson and for steering us in the right direction with regards to the Scottish Travellers. We wish to thank Routledge for the stories sourced from the late Katharine M. Briggs, whose magnificent *Dictionaries of British Folklore*, are like a holy book to us. Tony Robertson, thank you for your kind, generous response in sharing your father, Stanley Robertson's tale, 'Old Croovie', which we have retold here as 'Jack and the Dancing Trees'. Thank you James Spence for your advice regarding 'The Laddie who Herded Hares'. Eric Maddern, whose fleshed out version of the legend of St Baglan's Church 'The Tree with Three Fruits' is retold here, needs a special thank you for being an inspiration for environmental storytellers everywhere.

RE-ENCHANTING
THE WORLD

A CREATION STORY FOR OUR TIMES

'How did you put those pictures in my head?' the boy asked the storyteller, after a session of tales in his inner-city classroom.
'Through the magic of story,' she replied, smiling.

Once upon a time, stories wove the known universe together, connecting communities to each other, to the land where they lived and to the plants and animals they shared that land with. Local folk tales and legends belonged to the landscape they emerged from and to the people who lived there. These ties were particularly strong in the Celtic lands of England, Scotland, Ireland and Wales. Despite waves of immigration and cultural change, despite technological developments from the printing press to digital media, the threads of these bonds are still discernible in the myths and legends, ballads and folktales that have survived into the twenty-first century.

Storytelling and people evolved together. Our human brains are wired for the intimate connection of listening to someone tell a story. The simple words 'once upon a time' transport us to the archetypal hearth of our ancestors, a place where all humanity meets to share lasting wisdom. For most of human history, people carved stories out of raw experience as a way of creating truths to live by. Those tales that contained the wisest words were the ones that were remembered and retold, and remembered and retold down the centuries, until the printing press and the rise of science changed societies' relationship to narratives.

When Sir Isaac Newton, Sir Francis Bacon and their colleagues launched the scientific revolution, people began to tell new stories about the world around them and about their place in it. These stories began to separate people from the landscape and organisms around them, putting detachment and objectivity on a proverbial pedestal. As people became entranced with the shiny new things science could do, they stopped telling the old stories and they began to believe that people could live on a diet of cold hard facts and logic alone. Of course people went right on telling stories, but many of these stories were flimsy things, flat, not meant to last. People forgot that stories had once been quests for a good way to live, not just pleasant distractions for the end of the working day.

Lately, however, the stories emerging from the halls of science have been less than reassuring. The scientific community has become more and more concerned about the state of the world, outlining with increasing alarm the global crises the world is facing: deforestation, pollution, climate change, losses of habitat and accelerating rates of species extinction. Our earth is tired and drained. Robbed of enchantment, her abundant lands and oceans transformed into natural resources to be harvested and mined, she is on the verge of exhaustion. Their minds trained on screens for hours a day, people have forgotten that they are part of the earth and have ended up exhausted and depleted themselves.

For the better part of a hundred years, environmentalism pinned its hopes on technical rationality and technological fixes. However, in 1992 in Rio de Janeiro, with things still getting worse rather than better, the Earth Summit conceded that technical solutions alone were not going to move us to a sustainable future. The resulting Agenda 21 emphasised the need to facilitate shifts in peoples' attitudes and values as well. And what better way to bring this about than through stories.

What the world needs – what we need – is an infusion of storied magic to bring us back into life and back into the ecological community to which we belong. Fortunately, our foremothers and forefathers bequeathed us exactly what we need.

At the same time as attitudes and values were making it onto the environmental agenda, science was beginning to show that human brains are meant to do much more than process facts and complete logic puzzles. Since then, experimental psychology has shown that when people make decisions, they go to stories first, constructing narratives out of the situations they've found themselves in, and then relating these to the stories they have encountered. This is backed by neuroscience brain scans that demonstrate story is as essential to human life and reasoning as what we have come to know as facts and logic are. When it comes to values and attitudes, stories are even more central to human life.

Aristotle was the first to observe that a good society needs more than technical know-how. More than 2,000 years ago, he argued that in order for people to become good citizens, they also need practical wisdom. Recently, philosophers of ethics and psychologists of education have returned to Aristotle's writings, observing that practical wisdom is best developed through reflecting on personal experience through stories.

Facts alone will never be able to teach us how to love, because it is through story that we learn how to be in relationship with each other and with the world around us. Nor will facts ever be enough to show us how to live a good life, how to answer the question Socrates thought to be the most important question under the sun: How should I live?

If we are to learn how to live well, in harmony with each other and the other inhabitants of Earth, then we need more than facts. We need stories of wisdom and connection, love and magic. These days, we are used to finding stories in books, like this one, but once upon a time they only existed in people's memories. Each time a story was told, it would change slightly; another layer would be added through changing experiences, changing needs, changing audiences. In this way, the traditional tales that have come down to us are weighted with the insights of many tellings over many generations. A story that has lasted for centuries as a told tale has a certain substance to it, a multi-dimensionality that is lacking in so much contemporary culture. We feel the weight of these stories when we encounter them. The stories we have collected in this book have this kind of weight to them.

In the 1960s, for the first time, science sent men into outer space – achieving the greatest separation in relation to the planet that any human had ever managed before. These astronauts looked back at the planet that had birthed them and saw it, not with cool detachment, but with love. In the same period, James Lovelock invoked the old stories when he named his scientific theory of the interdependence of life on Earth after a goddess: the Gaia Hypothesis. Love and stories, we cannot escape them.

But before we get too nostalgic about stories, we need to remember that modern humans did not invent selfishness or cruelty. Wisdom stories are not the only tales that have been handed down from our ancestors. People do not always seek to know the truth. Too often they act out of greed or envy, fear or insecurity. As we trawled through archives, searching for tales to include in this collection, we sifted through stacks of folk traditions that justified the slaughter of very real birds and mammals, the cutting down of groves of old trees, and the scapegoating of other people for no good reason at all. Crows and wolves were the most consistently and viciously attacked by such traditions, but others including the cheerful yellowhammers and even little wrens suffered as well. Societies ruled by story alone can also be led down the wrong path.

What we need are the resources to tell stories that will support the sorts of shifts in attitudes towards nature that we know through science and rational thinking are needed, stories that can lead us on our journey towards a sustainable future. We hope that this collection will be one source of many for you to bring such stories into your life and your work.

This collection brings together tales from England, Scotland, Ireland and Wales. Many of these stories have their roots in Celtic traditions, which value connections with animals, plants and the land. Others travelled long distances before arriving in these parts and being transformed by local communities through the addition of local flora and fauna and the melding of cultures. All the stories in this collection invite tellers and listeners back into relationship with the more than human world in which we live. While based on traditional materials, we have retold these stories in the context of current environmental crises and in line with the goals of this book. They are weighted not only with the cumulative wisdom of the past, but also with our scientifically-informed knowledge of the present and our hopes for a future in which human communities come to live in harmony with the rest of the natural world.

FOLK TRADITION AND NATURE

At first I am as white as snow
Then as green as grass I grow
Next I am as red as blood
And finally as black as mud.
What am I?

(A riddle, learned from Scottish storyteller, David Campbell – the answer is: A bramble, or in English, a blackberry!)

The journey we took with this book began with a common interest in Celtic culture and an awareness – born out of our own storytelling practices – of the power of stories to connect people to the natural world. From this starting point, curiosity pulled us towards other strands of British folklore. Travellers' tales, Aesop, Norse epics, the Continental traditions of the Normans and those recorded by the Brothers Grimm all had an influence on the folk tales of England, Scotland, Wales and Ireland. And we soon discovered that they too had something to contribute towards nurturing an environmental sensibility. This collection, therefore, includes stories from a range of periods and traditions, all chosen for their ability to speak across cultures and centuries to contemporary global audiences. Given the diversity of sources, it is useful to know something of the background context. With this in mind, we will begin again with the Celts.

Celtic stories resonate with the natural environment that they emerged out of and the myriad life forms that dwell there. While each period of Celtic storytelling developed its own particular emphasis and style, they all shared a common weft of supernatural beliefs and magical powers, woven together with observations of nature and common sense, resulting in a tradition of stories that remain exciting and meaningful today. The central role of animals and nature in the Celtic world shaped and flavoured their stories, filling them with a rich source of environmental wisdom. That wisdom is the inspirational spark for this collection of stories.

The great age of Celtic pagan culture, when Celtic tribes covered great tracts of Northern Europe and the British Isles, span from around 600 bce to ce 400. These tribal cultures were very much bound to the land, seas, plants and animals around them. Their livelihoods of hunting, fishing, farming, herding, building, and crafting all depended upon nature's generosity and abundance.

Being so intimately tied to their environment, it is not surprising that these early pagan Celts focused their spiritual beliefs and holy practices on environmental forces, the landscape, and the creatures they lived amongst. These Celts worshiped every imaginable aspect of nature. Their most important divinities included the sun, moon, stars, thunder, fertility and water, but the landscapes they lived in were populated with all sorts of other deities who were attached to rivers, springs, boulders, rocks and mountains. Cults of celestial gods, the mother goddesses, water and trees were common to all of the different tribes, but plants, trees and animals also held important positions in Celtic life. Each was believed to possess its own spirit or numen, and all were respected and worshiped for their everyday and supernatural qualities.

This Celtic pagan religion was gradually replaced by Christianity and their stories might have been lost, had it not been for the early Christian monks who took an interest in Celtic culture. They wrote down many of their stories and sagas including creation myths, epic tales of supernatural heroes, and stories of pagan gods and goddesses, shape-changers and magical animals. It is thanks to the monks of

Ireland and Wales that we have the earliest written fragments of these stories, dating back to the sixth century ce. These ancient Celtic stories were told and re-told from one generation to the next and the monks' manuscripts were copied and re-copied from century to century, evolving as the dominant culture changed.

From the pagan period we have included two stories: 'Ceridwen's Cauldron' and 'Saving the Forest'. Ceridwen is from the Welsh tradition, a primeval mother, a moon-goddess from the oldest of the cyclical Celtic myths. In this story we witness her power as a shape-changer and are taken on a breathtaking chase as different animals hunt their quarries. Our re-telling of 'Ceridwen's Cauldron' helps us to explore the web of life in our own fragile eco-system.

Two faces of the Cailleach, another ancient Celtic goddess, feature in 'Saving the Forest', a story from Scotland. But there are also elements from Scandinavian culture in this story, which in one early source is titled 'The Norse King's Daughter'. The Viking influence in Scotland is reflected deeply through these old stories. In her youth this Celtic/Norse goddess is Bride, the goddess of spring and summer. Beara is the mature woman, the side of her which brings the dark months of the year and winter to the land. The story explores what happens when the seasons get out of balance, a lesson that is all too relevant to us today in this era of climate change. The story ends on a note of hope, with the wisdom of the young saving the day. All of the stories collected in this book reflect these basic values of respecting our fellow creatures and living in harmony with the world around us.

When Christian monks arrived in Ireland in the fifth century, they didn't just document the Celtic culture they found there, they absorbed a lot of its values, incorporating them into what is still known as Celtic Christianity. The early Christian saints of Ireland, Scotland and Wales were portrayed as having a special relationship with birds and animals and they continued the tradition of bardic nature poetry well into the twelfth century.

From the early Celtic Christian era we have included the stories of 'St Mungo and the Robin', 'St Brigid and the Wolf' and St Baglan and 'The Tree with Three Fruits'. The robin is also a popular figure in Scandinavian folklore; so again, a mixing of these traditions is in evidence.

St Baglan's story reminds us of the contributions that plants and animals make to human existence, while St Mungo provides a model of standing up to those who do not value life. St Brigid of Kildare, with her love of nature and her concern for the poor, is in many ways resonant with the more widely known St Francis of Assisi. Like the pagan stories before them, a great sense of reverence and love of nature is evident in these early Christian stories.

Through the Middle Ages, literary men and women – mostly monks and nuns – carried on transcribing Celtic stories from earlier periods and composing nature poetry. However, after this period, the literary tradition began to be replaced by more popular forms of storytelling. The bulk of our collection comes from this later, folkloric, period. Many of these folk tales may well have originated from much earlier pagan times, but the historical thread has been lost over the centuries.

By this period, Britain was already a multi-cultural space, with immigrant communities from a range of backgrounds meeting with and infusing earlier traditions with new stories and new ways of telling. These traditions would have included Aesop's fables, likely influences on the 'King and Queen of the Birds', which we have included here. When the Norman traditions met with the Celtic, King Arthur was born, represented here by the story of 'The Sleeping King'. Incomers from the forest regions of the continent would have met with the thriving forest-based communities here (partly represented by 'Saving the Forest') and new stories would have been born. We associate these forest stories mostly with the Brothers Grimm these days, but many of the stories here also demonstrate this sensibility. For example, we have included 'Magpie's Nest', a witty tale from England about how the birds learned to build their nests by copying the magpie, which is filled with real nest-building truths. Also, 'The Old Woman Who Lived in a Vinegar Bottle', a fantastical and funny campfire story about over-consumption and greed. This concept is as relevant for today's audiences as it was many generations ago.

From the earlier Celtic stories through to influences from Aesop, Christianity, Scandinavia, Continental Europe and beyond, all the stories collected here demonstrate a common wisdom for respecting nature and the other creatures we share these islands with. Stories travel, they have no respect for national borders and when they cross them, they have a tendency to morph into something new, to mingle and merge with local stories and, in general, to go about making themselves at home wherever they find themselves. Through bards, ballads, sailors, immigrants, travellers and grandparents, these stories have arrived on our shores and settled in our consciousness.

Several of the stories in this collection are from the Scottish Travellers' tradition – 'Jack and the Dancing Trees', 'Margaret McPherson's Garden', 'Archie's Besom', 'Seal Island' and 'Thomas the Thatcher'. These tales, like the Travellers themselves, are firmly linked to the land, the sea and to rural life. They deliver strong messages about respecting nature and living in harmony with the world.

The Travellers in Scotland are a nomadic people who have been recorded as living in Scotland since the twelfth century, but may have been present for much longer. They are a distinct ethnic group, believed to be descended from Northern European tribes.

In settled communities, the rising popularity of books, gramophones, radio, theatres and concert halls began to overtake folk storytelling traditions, all but wiping them out. However, the Traveller community maintained a complex, highly developed oral culture well into the twentieth century. During the 1950s students from the School of Scottish Studies in Edinburgh began recording and collecting their tales. Many anthologies are now in print, the most numerous being those of the late Duncan Williamson, edited by his wife Linda Williamson.

Until recently, the Travellers lived close to the land and many of their tales concern living in harmony with the Earth and its creatures. These stories are filled with environmental wisdom about taking what you need from nature while leaving enough berry, fish, tree, or wild animal stocks so that they can replenish themselves over the following years. A moral tone of modesty over greed is often found in these stories, which suits the contemporary environmental message well.

While their stories are grounded in a life lived in intimate relationship to Scotland's landscapes, plants and animals, the roots of these stories come from all over the place. The selkies and the fairy folk in the tales undoubtedly have Celtic roots, but Duncan Williamson himself thought 'Thomas the Thatcher' was a story that had originally come from the Netherlands. Meanwhile, 'Jack and the Dancing Trees' has deep resonances with stories told in the forested regions of the Czech Republic and Germany.

Largely through the generosity of Traveller storytellers such as Duncan Williamson, Stanley Robertson, Jess Smith, Sheila Stewart and many others, these stories have become core to the contemporary storytelling revival in Scotland and are, therefore, part of this collection no matter where they may have originally come from.

All of the tales in our collection connect us through their Celtic and folk roots with the natural world, on which our own existence depends. They have been discovered through careful digging and happy happenstance. Some we heard before we read them, others we only knew on the page before we began to tell them as part of our own storytelling repertoires. A few have been created from the tiniest tantalising scraps; others are stories that are well known here in the British Isles and are regularly told all over the world.

In the time-honoured tradition of oral storytelling, we have retold these stories with a twenty-first-century audience in mind and in the context of the environmental concerns of our time. Although they are told in our words, in keeping with our themes of respect and inter-dependence, we have included notes and telling-tips with each story, and full source information and comments at the back of the book. We have also included a guide to telling with the seasons and an index to the flora and fauna that makes an appearance in these stories.

This collection represents a contemporary take on a centuries-old Celtic and folk tale tradition of connecting to nature through careful observation and imaginative storytelling. It is our hope that these stories will travel far and wide, meeting with other stories and with other listeners and storytellers that share a reverence and love for this earth and her creatures.

May these stories speak to you not only of the past, but of a future in which people remember their interdependence with the rest of nature and seek to live in harmony with the world around them.

BRINGING STORIES TOGETHER

This book brings together two types of stories: traditional tales collected from a range of sources and the stories that each person carries with them about who they are and what their options are for being and doing in their lives. We want you to enjoy these stories, but more than this, we hope that these stories will do their work in the world by helping you, the reader, and anyone you share these stories with, to answer the important question, 'how should I live?' in ways that lead to sustainability for ourselves and the planet.

In the remainder of the book, we share our own retellings of some of our favourite stories from England, Ireland, Scotland and Wales. These may be read by yourself in silence. They may be read aloud to a group of pupils or a party of site visitors. Or, they may be told out loud.

Even if you have never done so before, we urge you to learn to tell some of these stories orally, without depending upon the words on the page. Something magical happens when stories are told in the old way. To tell a story is to create a sacred space, a space that contains not just you and your audience, but also all the other tellers and all the other listeners down through history. When we bring stories into our bodies and give voice to them, they become part of our lives. When we know a story by heart, we can connect more strongly with the people we are telling it to. As the Scottish Traveller saying goes: 'a story needs to be told eye to eye, mind to mind and heart to heart.' When we tell stories in this way, we connect emotionally with our audiences, we begin to create and to strengthen the bonds of community and we open up an opportunity for transformation to take place.

Storytellers conjure up worlds of adventure just by giving breath to words. In the hushed space between speaker and audience the stories form. The teller gives them shape, but the sensuous experience of story, the images, feelings, and emotional resonances, are supplied by the imaginations of the people listening, making it one of the best mediums for supporting individuality while building community.

Many excellent books have been published in recent years for beginner tellers. If you are new to this art form, we suggest you check out some of the books listed in the appendix. Even better, go out and find some live storytelling to listen to. The best way to learn is by watching a more experienced teller tell. Many communities across the world now have storytelling clubs, some of which even run courses for beginners.

The stories can be adapted to any age group from five-years of age to adults. A few, such as 'The Old Woman Who Lived in a Vinegar Bottle', will also appeal to younger children.

In days gone by, the audience response to a well told story would be silence, testimony that the listeners had been touched by what they had heard, were absorbing the message it brought to their lives and reflecting on their own experiences in light of these new narrative resources. Today's audiences will most likely clap after a story, which has the unfortunate effect of breaking the spell a few moments too early. They may need a little help in bringing their own personal experiences and stories together in ways that can facilitate reflection and even transformation. So, before closing a storytelling session, we suggest pausing first. Invite your audience to ask themselves the following questions:

1) What caught your imagination in the stories you just heard?
2) What does this connect with in your own life, either in the past or the present?
3) What new options does this story open up for being and acting in the world?

These questions help people get into the habit of using stories to reflect on their own lives. They can be encouraged to write their answers down or simply to contemplate them. You may then wish to have a discussion about what came up in their reflections. By moving from listening to reflecting, and only then to acting, people's learning will be deepened. Younger audiences can be helped to reflect through art. Ask children to make a picture of what they remember best, or liked best from the story they just heard. Then use their pieces of art to start a conversation.

Of course you are free, indeed encouraged, to use these questions yourself as you read through the stories in this book.

The stories we have collected cluster loosely into six categories. Those in 'Air' connect with the bird world and to flying, a source of fascination for people down the ages. While all of the birds in these stories are native to the British Isles, many are also found in other parts of the world. The stories in 'Fire' relate to the transformative potential of fire, for good and bad and to topics of energy and climate. 'Water' deals with creatures of rivers and of the sea, as well as with issues of access to drinking water and to conservation. 'Earth' stories take us into holes and caves as well as up into the air, through the power the soil has to make plants grow. The section on 'The Web of Life' presents a series of stories that explore some of the links between the various plants and animals of the British Isles, ending with a creation tale about compost! They are ecology stories. The final section, 'Living in Harmony', looks the most directly at how people might bring their lives into greater harmony with the rest of nature. Many of the stories in this section concern the feelings and attitudes we all struggle with that are tangled up with the overconsumption of the Earth's resources.

This is just what the stories have meant to us. One of the most powerful things about stories is that everyone gets something a little different out of them. For stories to live in the world, they must change and grow, so please make these stories your own.

Happy storytelling!

ABOUT THE AUTHORS

Allison and Alette met seven years ago at the Scottish Storytelling Centre on a day-long workshop about telling stories for Eco-schools. Despite our different backgrounds, we hit it off immediately, recognising in each other a kindred passion for using stories to heal the Earth.

The idea for this book emerged from conversations we began to have while Allison was working on her MA in Scottish Folklore. Her focus at the University of Glasgow was on tracing the threads of environmental values through folktales. For over a decade, Alette's research as a human geographer has examined the ways people use stories to make ethical decisions in relation to the places where they live and the natural world around them. As we talked, we discussed bringing these two areas of expertise together in a book that would highlight the contribution that homegrown stories from Scotland, England, Wales and Ireland can make to healing the Earth.

Over the last few years, Allison and Alette have been actively collecting traditional stories from the British Isles that speak to today's environmental issues. We have used most of these stories in our storytelling work with schools, libraries and organisations such as the Royal Zoological Society of Scotland, the Royal Botanic Garden Edinburgh, the Forestry Commission, and the Scottish Wildlife Trust.

With a degree in Drama Studies, Allison Galbraith embarked on a long and busy career in theatre, dance and education. While teaching drama and dance in Glasgow, Allison fell off a trapeze bar and left teaching to recover from her injuries. Her friends and dog walked her back to good health in the glorious, wild places of Scotland. Through her love of wildlife and habitat conservation, Allison focused her creative talents on stories and storytelling at such places as the Scottish Wildlife Trust's Falls of Clyde Nature Reserve and Glasgow Botanical Gardens. She joined the Scottish Storytellers' Directory in 2007 and has been working full-time as a teller and workshop leader ever since. In 2012, Allison completed a Master's degree in Scottish Folklore at Glasgow University.

Alette J. Willis has a PhD in Geography and Environmental Studies. She is a lecturer at the University of Edinburgh, where her research focuses on how people use stories to make sense of their lives and of the world around them. She has published academically on the integration of storytelling with outdoor education and wilderness therapy, as well as on how people use stories to make everyday ethical decisions in relation to plants, animals and the environment. Alette joined the Scottish Storytellers' Directory in 2011. She specialises in storytelling for science communication and is the Storyteller in Residence to the Royal Zoological Society of Scotland. Alette is a published author of fiction for adults and children. Her first novel for children, *How to Make a Golem (and Terrify People)*, was published by Floris Books in 2011.

AIR

MAGPIE'S NEST

(ENGLAND)

Once upon a time, a long time ago, birds did not build nests. They simply sat around on branches or boulders or even on the ground. And when it was time to lay eggs, they just laid them on a branch or a boulder or on the ground. Not many eggs survived.

Magpie began to think that there might be a better way of doing things.

She gathered branches from the forest floor, flew up into a tree and started to weave them together to form a nice round platform. It looked very comfortable and it would stop eggs from rolling out of trees. Pleased with herself, she landed in the middle of it.

The nest was not as comfortable as she'd imagined it would be. The knobbly sticks poked her ruthlessly.

Magpie decided that this was not the nest for her.

Crow, who had been watching what Magpie was doing, landed on the nest. She found it to be perfectly suited to her. To this day, Crow has been making her nest just the way Magpie did, weaving branches together into a shallow platform.

Magpie thought and thought about what she could find to make a nest softer. 'Aha!' She said, flying down to the riverbank. 'Mud is nice and soft, that's what I'll use to make my nest.'

Back up in a tree, Magpie made a simple platform of sticks. Then she flew down and scooped up a beak-full of mud, which she plopped down on her platform of sticks. She did this over and over again until she had a nice cake of mud. It looked very comfortable. But when she landed on the nest, it wasn't very comfortable at all. The mud was gloopy and it stuck to her feathers.

Magpie decided that this was not the nest for her.

Song Thrush, who had been watching what Magpie was doing, had an idea. She landed in the middle of the mud cake. Using her big belly, she began to shape that mud into a smooth, round bowl. To this day, Song Thrush has been making her nest out of sticks and mud.

Magpie thought and thought about what she could use to make a more comfortable nest. 'Aha!' she said, flying down to a patch of dried up long grass. 'I can weave my nest out of grass and straw and little tiny twigs.'

So that's what she did. When she was done, the nest looked nice and tidy … and tiny. She tried to land in it, but it was just too small.

Magpie decided that this was not the nest for her.

Blackbird, who had been watching what Magpie was doing, thought the nest looked perfect for her small family. To this day, Blackbird makes her nest by weaving together long pieces of grass and thin twigs.

Magpie thought that maybe she would be happier if she had a really big nest, with lots of room for herself and her eggs. She flew all about the forest picking up the longest sticks she could find. She wove them together into a huge platform. It looked wonderful, so spacious. She imagined how jealous the other birds would be now that she had such a humungous nest. She landed in the middle of it. One of the twigs on the far side of the nest popped out of place. She hopped over and fixed it. Immediately a stick on the other side came loose. She had to hop all the way across the huge nest to fix it.

Magpie decided it was just too much work having such a big nest.

Owl, who had been watching what Magpie was doing, thought the nest looked like a perfect place to raise owlets. To this day, this is how Owl makes her nest.

As Magpie thought and thought about how to make a more comfortable nest, it began to rain. 'I know what's missing,' she said. 'None of the nests I've made so far have had a roof on them. If I had a roof, everything would be exactly right.'

First she made a platform of sticks. Then, working very carefully, she built up the walls and wove together a roof. She left a hole in one wall, just big enough for her to slip through. Inside it was cosy and dry, but the bare sticks were still uncomfortable.

Long-Tailed Tit, who had been watching, thought that a domed nest would be perfect for her and her little family. She wove together a tiny dome of twigs. Then she gathered lichen from the trees and rocks and covered every inch of her nest with it. It kept out the wind and rain beautifully. To this day Long-Tailed Tit makes her nest this way.

Meanwhile, Magpie was busy finding things to make her nest more comfortable. She flew here and there collecting moss, grass, dried leaves, and sheep's wool. To make it even more snug and warm for her eggs, she pulled out some of the soft feathers on her own breast.

To this day, Magpie makes a domed nest out of sticks and lines it with all sorts of things, not just moss and feathers, but also scraps of cloth, yarn, and pieces of cardboard … she's still trying to make the perfect nest.

NOTES: This old English tale is a useful one to have in your repertoire for a drop-in storytelling event. Bring photos of birds and their nests to flip through as you tell the story, which takes about five minutes to tell. You can add and subtract species of birds from this story to make it more relevant to the region where you are telling it. You can also have your audience suggest what Magpie would use to make her domed nest more comfortable.

2

ARCHIE'S BESOM

(SCOTLAND, TRAVELLERS)

Once there were two brothers, Archie and Alex, who lived in the Highlands of Scotland. They farmed their own wee croft, but it was not large enough to support them, and so they had to take other work when they could find it. Alex was the oldest and he had always been the boss. He told Archie what chores to do each day and he was the one who collected the money from the people they worked for. Very occasionally, if the jobs had been particularly hard, like repairing farm roads, or building stonewalls, Alex would pay Archie sixpence. Even back in those days sixpence wasn't very much money, but Archie never complained.

One fine autumn morning, when the rowan trees were ripe with red berries and the swallows were circling high in the sky, getting ready to migrate south, the brothers had a job fixing an old stone dyke in a field next to a road. Archie was working away, putting the big stones into the wall and Alex was taking a nap in the shade of a tree. As Archie worked, a man walking down the road called out, 'Good day to you. Would it be all right if I picked some of that heather growing in your field over there?' The Travelling man pointed to the heather flowering all over the hillside.

'Aye, well the field is no' ours you see,' said Archie, 'we're just working here for the farmer who owns it. But I'm sure he would'ny mind you having a wee bit of the heather now. After all there's plenty of it!' Archie waved his hand across the sweep of the hillside, which was purple with heather blossoms.

The Traveller thanked him, jumped over the wall and with his pocketknife began to cut long, tough strands of the flowering plant. Archie watched, fascinated by the man's speed and skill with the sharp knife.

'What are you going to do with all that heather?' asked Archie.

'I'm going to make brooms with it,' said the man, 'you know, besoms for sweeping floors and steps and paths. Folk are ay' needing a good new besom at this time of year.'

'How do you make a besom?' Archie asked curiously.

'Well,' replied the Travelling man, 'you take a straight piece of wood, like a hazel branch, for the handle. Then you place the heather around one end, tie it on good and tight with string or wire, and shape the ends of the heather nice and tidy with your knife. Then you have a fine new besom!'

'How much do you sell one for?' asked Archie, who was beginning to have an idea.

'Och, sixpence a broom. But if you make one a wee bit bigger and smarter, why you can get a shilling for it!'

'A shilling!' gasped Archie, 'I've never earned that much money in my whole life! I'm lucky if he,' Archie pointed towards Alex, 'gives me a measly sixpence for a full week's hard work. And you can get that much for one wee besom! Do you mind telling me now, how long does it take to make one?'

The Traveller smiled at Archie and said, 'I can make a decent enough one in an hour or two.'

Archie's mouth fell open; this man could make more money for a couple of hours agreeable work than he made for a full week of backbreaking labour. Archie thanked the man for sharing his wisdom and watched as the Traveller bundled the heather under his arm and went on his way, off down the road.

Archie marched over to Alex.

'I quit!' he yelled.

His brother woke with a start.

'I quit!' yelled Archie again, to make sure his brother had heard him.

'What d'you mean, you "quit"?' asked Alex.

'I mean, I'm finished working for you,' said Archie. 'I'm not taking orders from you any more. And I'm not working for sixpence a week ever again!'

'What could you possibly do besides work for me?' Alex asked, looking puzzled.

'I'm going to make brooms just like the Tinker's and I'm going to sell them for sixpence a piece, and when I'm good at making them, I'll charge a shilling a broom!'

Alex started laughing at his brother. 'You can't make besoms like a Tinker can. They're skilled craftsmen. They started learning from their parents and grandparents when they were still wee bairns. Besides, what do you need money for? You live in the house with me and I buy all the food and pay for it.'

'I'll do whatever I like with my money!' Archie was so angry he turned away from his brother and strode off towards home.

Along the way, he cut a great big bundle of bushy heather and found some good stout tree branches. He took these into the barn and set about making his very first besom. He tried to do it just as the Traveller had described, laying the fronds of heather tightly next to each other all around the pole. He bound the bundle on securely with good copper wire, and then sliced the pointy tips of the heather off with a sharp knife.

When he had finished, he stood back to admire his besom. It was quite a thing to see. Archie had used almost twice as much heather as the Tinker had collected that day. But the thing was, the Travelling man was going to make at least three or four brooms out of what he'd collected, and

Archie had made just one. But Archie was in too much of a hurry to think about how big his besom was. He set off immediately to see if he could sell it.

He walked for many miles, knocking on every door he came to. But no one wanted to buy his besom. Some told him they'd bought one already from the Tinkers. Others just laughed in his face, saying it was far too heavy to sweep with.

Carrying his enormous broom, Archie walked further than he had ever gone before, far beyond all the farms and houses he knew. He was almost ready to give up when he noticed a white cottage high on the hillside. His heart lifted. He doubted if the Travelling folk would have bothered going all the way up there to sell their goods.

Archie climbed the hill and knocked on the door. A very big woman with rosy cheeks answered. When she saw Archie's besom, her face lit up.

'Well lad, that's the biggest, finest besom I've ever seen! How much do you want for it?'

Archie explained that since it was the first he had ever made, a sixpence would be plenty.

The woman, whose name was Big Mags, took the broom from Archie and had a good look at it.

'It's excellent, I'll buy it!' She took a very shiny sixpence out of a little wooden box and handed it to Archie. She leaned close to his ear and whispered, 'Now laddie, that's a special sixpence. Every time you use it, you'll find a new silver sixpence has appeared in your wallet to replace the one you just spent.'

Archie couldn't believe his luck, a magic sixpence! He gave Big Mags a careful look and thought he could see a special sparkle in her eyes. He thanked her and hurried back to the village to see if the coin she'd given him really worked. If it did, he'd be free from his brother for good.

Big Mags was indeed special, just like the coin she'd given Archie. You see, Big Mags was a witch – the biggest witch that ever lived in Scotland. Some folk called her 'stout', or 'big-boned', and nasty ones called her 'fat', but most people got on with her just fine, because of her kind and friendly nature. The only people that didn't like Big Mags were the other witches. They hated her. They said cruel things about her size, because they were jealous of her happy disposition and magical powers. She could out-spell and out-charm each and every one of them. Big Mags used her supernatural gifts only for good, and this made them even angrier and nastier to her.

Mags decided it was time to teach them all a lesson. It was almost Hallowe'en and the local witches would be gathering in a clearing in Birch Tree Woods, for their special celebration. She hadn't been to a Hallowe'en party for years, because she could never find a broom big enough to carry her. But now she had one, Archie's besom!

Mags conjured up a spectacular broomstick spell and just before midnight on Hallowe'en, off she flew, high up into the air, riding her magnificent new besom. She sailed through the sky, and then hovered over Birch Tree Woods. She could see all the other witches arriving; their brooms looked very small and skinny compared to hers. As she whizzed down through them, they fell and scattered to the left and right. When they saw who it was they looked very unhappy and started whispering:

'Who invited that big lump?'

'Oh no, it's the Massive Maggot!'

'Drat! Goody-fat shoes is here, hide!'

'Don't mind me,' said Big Mags, 'I'm just here to have some Hallowe'en fun.'

She began to chant a strange little incantation in the Gaelic language. As she finished saying the spell, all of the broomsticks belonging to the other witches leaped into the air, bucking off their owners. The empty brooms circled once, twice, three times around the witches' heads, then rocketed up into the air, landing high up in the branches of the birch trees. And that's where they stayed. There was nothing the witches could do to get their brooms back, because Big Mag's magic was so much stronger than theirs.

Big Mags flew back to her cottage on her new super-broom, laughing all the way.

Meanwhile, the miserable, mean witches had to walk miles and miles through bogs and mud to get home. Mags had taught them a lesson they would never forget.

To this day, if you look up into the branches of birch trees, you can still see those witches' brooms stuck there. They look a bit like twigs in a crow's nest, but look closer and you will see that they really are witches' besoms, and now you know how they got there!

NOTES: Have you ever looked up into the branches of a birch tree and seen a tangle of twigs that resembles a crow's nest? These strange growths are known as Witches' Brooms and a mature birch tree can have up to a hundred of them. Witches' Brooms are caused by the fungus Taphrina betulina, which penetrates the tree and causes it to grow a cluster of extra shoots. The growth is called a gall and it does not harm the tree in any significant way. In Britain these galls usually only happen in birches, but in other parts of the world they can appear on elms, pines and other species of tree. People used to believe that these growths appeared because witches had flown over the trees.

This is a story which the famous Scottish storyteller and Traveller, Duncan Williamson liked to tell, especially around Hallowe'en. 'Besom' is the Scots word for broom.

This is a great story to tell on a woodland walk, especially when you can see the Witches Brooms in the birch trees. Take your own home-made broom. You could even make an extra big one like Archie's.

THE LADDIE WHO HERDED HARES

(SCOTLAND AND ENGLAND, BORDER REGION)

Once upon a time, there was a widow who lived in a little cottage with her two sons. Times were tough, it was hard to find work and often they had to go without a meal.

One day, the eldest son came to her and said that it was time he left the valley to go and seek his fortune elsewhere. The widow sighed sadly, but she knew that children must grow up, so she gave him a sieve and an old cracked bowl and told him to go down to the stream and fill them with water. She would use whatever water he brought back to make a bannock bread for his journey.

The eldest son took the sieve and the old cracked bowl and went down to the stream. A little bird, perched on the end of a reed growing at the water's edge, sang merrily to the bright blue sky. But as soon as he saw the young man carrying the sieve and the cracked bowl he changed his tune:

Stop it with moss and clog it with clay,
And then you'll carry the water away.

'Stupid creature. Telling me what to do! I'll not get my hands covered in dirt and moss, just because you tell me to. Be gone,' the eldest said, shooing him away, 'Leave me to do things my own way.'

He leaned down and dunked the sieve and the bowl in the water, filling them to the brim. But as soon as he took them out of the stream, the water flowed out again. He tried a couple more times. Finally, he dunked them in, took them out, and ran as fast as he could back to the cottage.

The widow looked at the few drops still clinging to the bottom of the sieve and the bowl and sighed. But she set to work, baking her eldest son a tiny, wee bannock. He was in such a hurry to be off, that he left without thanking her or saying goodbye to his brother.

He walked to the east; he walked to the west. He walked north; he walked south. He walked up hills and down, along roads and across fields, until he was too weary to go on. He sat down under a birch tree to eat his wee bannock. No sooner had he sat down, but the little bird landed on a branch above him.

He glared at the bird, but the bird sang his cheerful song anyway. 'Give me a bite of your bannock and I'll let you pluck a feather from my wing so you can make yourself a pair of pipes,' said the bird.

'Stupid creature. Telling me what to do!' said the eldest son. 'What would I want a pair of stupid pipes for? I'm off to seek my future. Besides, it's all your fault that I have only this tiny bannock to eat. There's barely enough for me, I'm not wasting any on you.' He shooed away the bird and crammed the rest of the bannock in his mouth, finishing it in two bites.

Then up he got and away he walked, seeking his fortune. He walked to the east; he walked to the west. He walked north; he walked south. He walked up hills and down, along roads and across fields, until at last he came to a grand house, where the king lived.

This is the place for me, he thought, and in he went to ask if they had any work for a young man of fine strength and character such as himself.

'What can you do?' asked the king.

'I can chop your wood and sweep your floors and look after your cattle,' said the eldest son.

The king waved his hand dismissively. 'I've got plenty of help with all of those things,' he said. 'What I need is someone who can herd hares. Can you do that?'

Herding hares? The eldest son knew about herding sheep and looking out for cattle, but never had he heard of herding hares. How hard could it be?

'Certainly,' he said. 'I can herd hares.'

'Excellent,' said the king. 'You will start tomorrow. If you bring them all back safely at the end of the day, I'll let you marry my daughter.'

'That suits me fine,' said the eldest son, thinking how easy it was going to be to make his fortune and marry a princess to boot.

'Good,' said the King. 'But if you don't bring them all home safe and sound, I'll hang you.'

The eldest son did not like the sound of that, but it was too late now. Besides, he was quite confident he'd be able to herd hares. After all, they were small and didn't have much going on in their heads.

The king sent him off to a room with no mention of supper. His stomach was grumbling, he'd walked far and only eaten one tiny bannock all day. But as soon as he was in bed, he fell soundly asleep.

He woke late the next morning and hurried downstairs to find the king had eaten all the porridge and the bannocks and drunk all the tea. The king offered him a glass of water and sent him out to watch the hares in a nearby field.

There were four and twenty hares, plus a wee lame one, playing amongst the long grass and meadow flowers. The eldest son sat down grumpily. Here he was, sent out to work under the hot sun with nothing to eat, even though he had been singled out to marry the king's daughter.

As he sat, watching the hares, his stomach growling louder and louder, he noticed how plump and well fed the beasts were. Surely the king would not begrudge him one. After all, the king had as good as promised him his daughter's hand.

The eldest son jumped to his feet and lunged after the nearest hare. It hopped out of his reach. He ran after another one, but it was faster than he. Finally, his eyes fell on the little lame hare. He grabbed it before it could bolt, broke its little neck, skinned it and roasted it over a fire. After his meal, he felt sleepy, so he napped in the long grass, amongst the meadow flowers, while the remaining hares cowered in the far corner of the field.

When he woke up, the sun was setting and it was getting cold. He tried to the catch the hares, but they had seen what he had done to their friend and they scattered in front of him, dashing of in all directions. He tried for hours, but could not catch a single one. He tried whistling. He tried coaxing them with dandelion leaves. He tried shouting at them. But they would not come anywhere near him.

In the end he returned to the grand house alone.

The king was waiting.

'Did you watch over my hares?' asked the king.

'Yes sir,' said the eldest son.

'Then where are they?' asked the king.

'I had to leave them in the field. They kept running away from me,' replied the eldest son.

'Even the wee lame one?' asked the king.

'No sir, I hadn't been given any supper or breakfast so I caught and ate the wee lame one,' he replied.

'Hang him,' cried the King angrily. And that's what they did.

A year and a day later, back in the wee cottage in the valley with the stream, the youngest son came to his widowed mother to tell her that he was going out into the world to see what kind of life he could make for himself. She sighed, but she knew that children must do what children must do. She got out the sieve and the old broken bowl and told him to fill them from the stream, and she would make him a bannock to take with him on the journey.

He could hear the sweet sound of bird song as he approached the stream. A pretty little bird perched on a bramble branch that reached out over the clear, running water. As soon as the bird saw him and what he was carrying, he changed his tune:

Stop it with moss and clog it with clay,
And then you'll carry the water away.

The youngest son looked at the bright-eyed little bird and laughed. 'You're a clever one aren't you?' he said. 'Thank you for your help.'

He collected moss and lined the bottom of the sieve with it. Then he covered the moss with clots of clay and smoothed it down until it was sealed. He did the same with the crack in the bowl. Carefully, he filled both vessels with water and carried them home. He didn't spill a drop.

His mother was pleased when she saw how much water he'd brought. With it, she baked him a huge bannock. He thanked her and kissed her on the cheek. She gave him her blessing and off he went to make a life for himself in the big, wide world.

He walked to the east; he walked to the west. He walked north; he walked south. He walked up hills and down, along roads and across fields, until at last he was weary and he sat down under a birch tree to eat his bannock. No sooner had he sat down, but the little bird landed on a branch above him.

'Hello, old friend,' said the young man. 'What can I do for you?'

'Give me a wee bite of your bannock and I'll let you pluck a feather from my wing so you can make yourself a pair of pipes,' said the bird.

'You can have as much bannock as you like,' said the youngest son, crumbling some up for the bird and laying it on the ground. 'After all it is because of you that I have such a big bannock. But I'll spare you your wing feathers. I wouldn't want to hurt such a beautiful creature.'

The bird hopped down and pecked up all the bannock crumbs. The youngest son crumbled up some more, ate a few more bites himself, and then wrapped up what remained.
The bird stopped pecking, stretched out one of his wings and looked up at the young man with his bright, beady eyes. 'Please take one of my wing feathers. It won't hurt me a bit. Consider it a gift.'

The young man knew it was rude to refuse a gift. Reluctantly he took hold of one of the bird's feathers. It pulled out easily. The bird finished eating the crumbs and flew off, trilling his cheerful song as he went.

Using his knife, the youngest son trimmed the feather, cut the shaft in two and notched it.

Bringing the pipes to his lips, he began to play the cheerful little song the bird had been singing. It made his feet feel like dancing. So he danced.

He danced to the east; he danced to the west. He danced to the north; he danced to the south. He danced up hills and down, along roads and across fields, until at last he came to a fine house, where the king and all his household lived.

Night was drawing in and he was weary, so he thought he'd stop at the house and see if there was any work to be had for a willing lad. He went in and was greeted by the king.

'What can you do?' asked the king.

'I can chop your wood and sweep your floors and look after your cattle,' said the youngest son.

'I've already got plenty of help with all of those things,' said the king. 'I need someone to herd my hares. Can you do that?'

Herding hares? The youngest son knew about herding sheep and looking after cattle, but never had he heard of herding hares. It sounded like it might be fun.

'I've never herded hares before,' he said, 'but if that's what needs doing, I'll do my best.'

'Excellent,' said the king. 'You can start tomorrow. If you bring them all back to the house, safe and sound, you can marry my daughter.'

'That would suit me,' said the youngest son, 'as long as it suits her.'

'Hrumph,' said the King. 'What suits my daughter is none of your business. You just worry about taking care of my hares. If you do not bring them all back safely, I'll see you hanged.'

The youngest son did not like the sound of that, but it was too late now. No mention was made of supper, so when he got to the room he'd been given, he unwrapped the rest of his bannock, broke it in two, ate one piece and wrapped up the other. He went to bed happy and content.

The next morning he came downstairs only to find that the king had eaten all the porridge and bannock and drunk all the tea. He drank the glass of water he was offered and went off to the nearby field to find the hares.

There were four and twenty hares frolicking in the tall grass, amidst a rainbow of meadow flowers. A wee lame one watched them, twitching her nose happily. The young man sat down, took out the rest of his bannock and ate it slowly while he watched them play. He thought to himself that there could be no better life than this, to sit in the sun and watch over these happy creatures.

He took out his pipes and began to play, his fingers finding the notes of the bird's cheerful song. The hares stopped playing, their long ears turning towards the clear sound of the pipes. As the song played on, they started to sway and dance, circling around the young man.

The song carried far and wide. Fish swimming in the river heard it and lay still to listen. Ducks in the pond stopped paddling, and bobbed on the tranquil water, their eyes half-closed. Everywhere peace reigned. The hawks flying high in the sky heard it, left off their hunting and came back down to earth so that they might hear it better. Flies buzzed sleepily amongst the heather flowers. Dragonflies came to rest on the lily pads.

The only creatures that moved were the hares. All afternoon the young man played and all afternoon they danced. Only when the sun was beginning to lower in the western sky, did he put his pipes away.

The fish in the river shivered and swam on. The ducks woke and began their quacking gossip. The hawks and dragonflies lifted back into the air. Only then did the hares stop dancing.

'It's time for us to go home now,' he said to the hares. He started off across the field, the four and twenty hares following after him, but the little lame one was nowhere to be seen.

The young man returned to the circle of matted-down grass that the hares had made in their dancing and there he found her, too tired to move. He picked her up gently in his arms. 'Don't worry, little one,' he said. 'I'll get you home and safe to bed.' She looked up at him with liquid brown eyes and he smiled down at her.

He led the four and twenty hares into the barn, but the littlest one he took to his own room, so that she might sleep on a feather bed, instead of the hard dirt floor. Then he went downstairs to meet with the king.

'Where are my hares?' asked the king.

'They are safely in the barn,' said the young man.

The king strode over to the barn and threw the door open. Four and twenty pairs of brown eyes shone out at him. 'Where's the littlest one?' asked the king, angrily. 'I told you to look after all of them.'

'She seemed very tired,' said the young man. 'I took her up to my room, so that she might sleep in comfort.'

'Hrumph,' said the king. He strode up the stairs to the young man's room and flung open the door.

A beautiful young woman lay on his bed; she opened her eyes and gazed at the young man with liquid brown eyes.

'You've watched over my hares, brought them all back safely and found my daughter,' said the king. 'You may now marry her.'

'Only if she will have me,' said the young man.

'Hrumph,' said the king.

'Let me think about it,' said the princess.

'Why don't I play you some music, while you think,' said the young man, pulling the pipes from his pocket. He put them to his lips and began to play the bird's cheerful little song. Everyone in the great house stopped what they were doing and started to dance. The king began to prance about. The princess got up off the bed and swayed and twirled, no trace of a limp in her steps.

All night long the entire household danced and laughed and made merry.

When the sun rose the next morning, the young man put away the pipes and the princess took his hand.

'I have thought about it,' she said, 'and I believe that being married to you would suit me just fine.'

They all lived happily ever after.

NOTES: The hare is a magical animal in Celtic lore, most often associated with the moon. In this story, the king might be understood as the sun and his daughter, the hare-princess, as the moon. The solar year is a bit longer than twelve moon-cycles long. So the twenty-four hares plus one can be understood as the full and new moons over the course of the year. The first son ignores the messages that the other creatures of the land are trying to tell him, so he goes hungry and eventually angers the sun-king. The second son shows respect for nature and her creatures and so returns the world to balance and joy.

4

KING AND QUEEN
OF THE BIRDS

(ENGLAND, IRELAND, SCOTLAND, WALES)

One day, the birds were all gathered together in the woods, discussing which of them was the prettiest, the handsomest, the strongest and the cleverest. The wise owl shouted for silence and suggested that rather than bickering and arguing, they should have a competition, whoever won would be crowned the King and Queen of the birds.

The birds agreed that this was a good idea, but once again they started arguing over what sort of competition it should be. Each species suggested a competition that would favour their own special skills and talents.

A strong, loud voice from the back boomed out, 'We should have a competition to see who can fly the highest.' It was one of a pair of eagles who had spoken. All the other birds shook and shivered in fright but they all agreed. Well, they didn't dare argue with an eagle!

So it was decided that they would meet the next day to hold a flying contest.

The birds gathered the following morning at dawn. They had all eaten a filling breakfast to give them energy for the competition: the sparrows had pecked plenty of grass seeds, the robins had gorged themselves on caterpillars and the buzzards had scoffed lots of plump voles. As each bird arrived, they sang their own unique tune, stretched their wings and fluffed up their feathers in readiness for the great event.

The collared doves and wood pigeons sang out together, 'On your marks, get set, go! On your marks, get set, go! On your marks, get set, GO!' (They always repeated themselves at least three times!)

A wave of rushing wind swept the woodland as each bird beat its wings and took flight. The contest to see who could fly the highest had begun.

The birds flew up into the sky until they got as far as their wings would take them. The littlest birds flew just past the treetops, but then had to give up and return to the ground, because their small wings were exhausted. Bigger birds flew high into the clouds before becoming too tired to continue. But two birds soared further than any of the others. It was the golden eagles.

They glided on the thermals of air, circling above the other birds. They flew so far that breathing was difficult – the air is thin, high in the atmosphere above Earth.

As these great birds looked down on all the others, who were giving up, one by one, they shouted out triumphantly, 'We have won. We have gone higher than any other bird!'

'Not so fast,' peeped a voice. With a fluttering of tiny wings, two little brown birds flew out from their hiding place amongst the feathers on the eagles' backs. The two birds hovered a few inches above the eagles and squeaked, 'Look, who has flown the highest now? We are the winners!'

The eagles turned their heads, staring in disbelief at the tiny stowaways who were barely managing to keep alight above them. It was the jenny wrens!

The eagles were furious at being outsmarted by such insignificant birds. They screeched angrily, swooping away towards earth. The little wrens chirped in delight, until they thought about what a long way back down it was.

The eagles tossed them off and the wrens began their descent, the wind racing through their wings. They fell faster and faster, until thump, thump, the poor creatures hit the ground so hard that their tail feathers were pushed upwards out of their rumps – and still to this day the wren's tail points straight up at the sky.

All of the other birds waiting below cheered for the wrens. They had won the competition through their wit and cleverness, not through great size or strength.

And so, it was the clever, tiny wrens that were crowned King and Queen of the birds.

NOTES: This story makes a very appealing introduction to the study of birds and their habitats. Wrens are the second smallest bird in Britain – the goldcrest is the smallest.

When telling this story; at the point where the birds begin to argue about what type of competition to hold, you can ask the listeners to say what their favourite bird is, and why it should be crowned King or Queen of the birds. If the eagle is suggested too early on, say you will come back to that bird, because it is so special. You can give all of the different birds in the story voices and have fun with accents, pitches and dialogue. Making bird-masks and turning the tale into a drama can be fun too.

FIRE

5

CERIDWEN'S CAULDRON

(WALES)

Ceridwen, the ancient moon goddess and mother of our planet, gave birth to twins, a girl and a boy. Her daughter, Creirwy was a beauty but the boy, well, dark hair covered most of his little body. His mother named him Avagddu, 'black wings', because his dark, soft down reminded her of a raven's magnificent, blue-black feathers. She thought he was the most wonderful boy alive. But as Avagddu grew, it became plain to Ceridwen that she alone thought him attractive. He wasn't very good at his school lessons either and the goddess tired of hearing others' rude whispers about how ugly and stupid her son was. She decided to use her knowledge of magical plants and herbs to help him.

She gathered the roots of certain plants that would stop unwanted body hair from growing, flowers which could lighten skin, and nectar to make eyes clear and bright. She placed these herbs in her great iron cauldron, mixed in pure spring water, and placed the pot over a fire of apple wood and hazel branches. After much stirring and gentle simmering, the brew was ready and Ceridwen poured the elixir into Avagddu's bedtime milk.

But, after he drank it, things took a turn for the worse. His eyes did shine more brightly, but his odd little face became even darker and hairier than before! More children began to tease him and unkind adults talked openly about, 'that foolish, hairy crow-boy'. His mother became more determined than ever to make a remedy to cure her son's problems. Her herb-lore was vast; she knew that if she collected all the sacred plants in the world and brewed them in her magical cauldron for one year and a day, she would have a medicine to make her child the most handsome and intelligent boy on earth. So, Ceridwen set out to gather these plants.

She crossed all the oceans and seas, trekked through dusty deserts, tramped through dark forests and climbed tall mountains. Each root, seed, herb and flower she found was lovingly brought back home to Wales and put into her cauldron. While the goddess was away, her neighbour's young boy, Gwion, was left to look after the cooking. He had been shown how to keep the pot heating gently and how to stir carefully and slowly with a long spoon made of walnut wood.

Gwion knew that this herb-soup was very special and very important and that whatever happened he was, 'NEVER TO TASTE IT!' Ceridwen had made him promise not to let the brew pass his lips. If it did, she would have him killed.

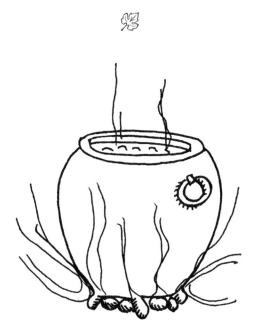

Now, one year and one day is a long time for a young boy to sit tending a fire and stirring a big pot of soup. A few times he fell asleep and nearly let the fire go out, but he always managed to rekindle the flames just in time to keep the potion simmering in the cooking pot. Once, he even dropped the spoon in the pot. He had to fish it out with a long twig, being careful to prevent any splashes from escaping.

Finally, the day arrived when the mystical liquid was ready. Gwion waited for Ceridwen to return. He knew she would arrive on the wind and conduct a magical ceremony involving the bubbling liquid in her cauldron. Then she would give the elixir to her child, Avagddu. But something awful happened – as Gwion gave one final stir to the steaming potion, three drops of hot liquid splashed, hissing, out of the pot and landed on his finger. They scalded his skin. He yelled in pain, and without thinking, stuck his sore finger into his mouth to sooth the burn.

In that instant, Gwion was transformed from a boy to a man, from a student to a wise teacher. He knew that all of the magical essence of the brew had been contained within those three little drops, now all the wisdom of the world was in him. What was left in the cauldron was deadly; even breathing in the fumes would kill a person. An ear-splitting crack made Gwion jump, as the giant cauldron broke in two. He leaped away, just managing to avoid the poisonous concoction as it poured out of the shattered container. Gwion fled from Ceridwen's house, fearing what she would do to him when she discovered that he had stolen the gift intended for her son.

All too soon, Ceridwen returned. She saw immediately that Gwion was gone and that all that was left in her broken cauldron was a deadly brew of poison. Gathering herself up into the sky in a dark storm cloud of fury, she vowed to hunt Gwion down and kill him.

With a sinking heart, Gwion saw the storm cloud grow. It would have been impossible for a normal man or woman to escape from the angry goddess, but Gwion had his new superpowers of wisdom and intelligence – now he had a slim chance of outwitting Ceridwen and escaping her vengeance.

'What is the fastest thing in the world?' he asked himself. The answer blew back to him in the air.

'Of course.' Gwion changed himself into a gust of wind and sped away from the angry goddess. He blew for many miles, but eventually grew too tired to continue in that form. He stopped to rest, but the furious shrieks of Ceridwen's thundering storm cloud drew rapidly nearer.

He turned himself into a fine, fast hare, and ran for his life. But Ceridwen was also a shape-shifter and she changed into a sleek greyhound. In a moment, she closed in on the hare, her sharp white teeth gnashing, ready to rip and kill her prey.

Feeling the dog's hot breath on his fur, Gwion leaped into the river and turned himself into a strong, silver fish. The powerful ripples of his body took him quickly downstream, away from the snarling dog. But the clever goddess turned into an otter and dived into the water in pursuit of her prey. Gwion saw the flash of wet fur and two black eyes staring into his. The otter opened its mouth to bite. Gwion changed into a tiny bird, flying with all his might out of the river and into the bushes. He darted and fluttered under branches, between the thorns. The goddess leaped out of the river, turning herself into a mighty hawk, swooping after the little bird.

Gwion's tiny bird heart beat so fast he feared it might pop. The hawk's razor-sharp talons tore at the branches above him. In desperation, he left the bushes and flew through the open door of a farmer's barn. His body crashed into a pile of grain. This gave Gwion an idea. He turned himself into a single grain of wheat. Here at last, buried amongst thousands of other grains, he must surely be safe from the angry goddess!

But nothing could deceive a supernatural being as clever and powerful as Ceridwen, moon goddess and mother of all. She changed into a plump, black hen and pecked with great delight at all of the grain in the barn. Eventually Gwion too was swallowed up, disappearing inside her belly.

There he stayed for nine months, growing as a new life inside the all-powerful goddess.

Ceridwen was annoyed that she was carrying this boy, a child who had tricked and deceived her. She planned to kill him, but when he was born, she was amazed by his perfect beauty – she couldn't slay this gorgeous, little, baby boy. Instead, she wrapped him carefully inside a soft cloth, placed him in a strong leather bag, then set him to float on the sea in a small coracle, woven from water reeds.

The next day, the boat drifted ashore many miles away. A washer-woman found the baby and took him home. Her husband thought he was a fine little boy. Together they named him Taliesin and they brought him up with much kindness and love.

Taliesin had many adventures during his life and grew up to be the most skilled storyteller of all. His tales are still shared and enjoyed today, because everyone loves a good story.

NOTES: This tale contains an exciting chase scene, which is an excellent illustration for the chain of life. Medicinal plants are another subject contained within this tale. The story can be told as a fun introduction to the topic of plant medicine and herbal preparations.

6

THE ALDER SPRITE

(ENGLAND)

Tam lived in a cottage, near a very special well called the Saints' Well. All the water he ever needed came from this well. Tam knew how lucky he was to live next to such a wonderful source of water. It was the clearest, purest water in the whole valley – in fact many folk said it was the best water in the whole of Somerset! Even on hot summer's days it stayed cool and untainted. Tam used the well like a larder, keeping his butter, cheese and even his salt bacon in a bucket down the well. He was one of the few people in the village whose pork was still fresh enough to eat in the winter; safely preserved in the dark, cold well. Each year Tam ate juicy pork, with crispy crackling for his Christmas dinner, such a rare treat in those days before refrigeration, and all thanks to the Saint's Well.

An alder tree grew next to the well – it had been there as long as Tam could remember. One summer, when its leaves were full and bright green, he noticed that one of the tree's lower branches was growing right across the mouth of the well, making it harder for Tam to draw the water up in his bucket. He muttered and grumbled about the encroaching limb, but Tam knew full well that it was a very unwise thing to cut an alder. None of the old folk in the valley would ever prune such a sacred tree; rumour had it that the tree would bleed if cut and awful things would happen to the person who harmed it.

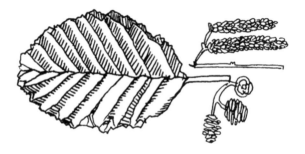

As summer ended and autumn turned the land from green to gold, the leaves began to drop down into the water. Tam swore that the fallen leaves were causing the water to taste sour. Finally, he decided to cut off the limb.

'Surely chopping one branch wouldn't offend any spirits?' he thought to himself.

He took his axe, sharpened the blade and began to chop at the branch. To Tam's surprise, a loud moan escaped from the branches above his head. He stopped and looked up into the tree's canopy. He was horrified to see wood smoke swirling through the leaves. He turned to his house; he hadn't lit a fire yet today. He ran up the path just to be sure the house was all right. When he got to his property, all was fine, no smoke, no fire – it must have been his imagination.

Tam returned to his job, chopping off the low branch above his precious well. As he raised his axe high and brought it down forcefully into the bark, there came an even louder cry from the very heart of the tree. Now Tam heard fire crackling and even caught a whiff of the unmistakable smell of burning. Again he dropped the axe and ran to his cottage, terrified that somehow his thatch or timbers were alight. And once more he saw everything was fine, the cottage was standing as it should be – no fire, or burning timbers.

'Right!' Tam said angrily. 'I'm being tricked by some spirit here, or else I'm losing my mind. I'm not going to pay attention to anymore of this nonsense, or witchery!'

He went back to the well, picked up his axe and chopped at the branch for all he was worth. Each time the blade struck into the wood, a piercing scream rang out. With each blow of the axe, the terrified tree spirit cried louder and louder. Tam heard the cries of pain and smelled wood smoke. He heard flames beginning to leap and rise, crackling and hissing, as if a fire began to rage behind him.

'Oh, no, you're not foolin' me again. I'm not paying any mind to your trickery. I'm taking this limb off and that's that!'

Despite the sound, smell, and now heat of a raging house-fire, Tam kept on with his task until the long, leafy branch lay on the ground, severed from the body of the tree.

Tam picked up his prize with pride. It was a good, solid piece of wood and Tam smiled to himself as he thought how well it would burn in his hearth tonight. But as he turned to take it up to his log-pile, he saw red-faced neighbours and villagers running towards his cottage.

'Fire, fire!' they yelled, as more villagers came running with buckets of water to put out the blaze.

Tam reached his house too late. This time the flames were real, the whole place was ablaze. There was nothing Tam or his neighbours could do to stop the fire from destroying his home.

A very sorry Tam sat down in the dirt, still holding the alder branch, and sobbed. A kindly lass gave him a mug of water from the well, and when he could talk, he told the villagers about the visions the tree-spirit had given him, and how he had foolishly ignored them.

The local folk looked on in pity but all agreed that the alder sprite had given him fair warning and poor Tam had got his just desserts.

NOTES: The ancient Celtic tribes believed that trees were magical, and none more so than the alder tree. This is the type of wood used by water-diviners when they are looking for underground water. Slender alder branches are held lightly in the diviners' hands, and start to twitch and pull downwards when they pass over the hidden water source; the spirit of the wood is thirsty for a drink of subterranean water.

Because of its never-ending thirst, the tree always grows near water.

This West Country story echoes these old beliefs. Tam knew it was a sacred tree, not to be cut, but he ignored the warnings, suppressed his own instincts and emotional intelligence. The result was a simple direct lesson about respecting the life of the tree and Tam paid with his home.

The theme of spirits living in trees is common in British and European folklore and throughout the world. The Celtic lunar calendar attributed a specific tree to each lunar month – this was your lucky tree. This is where the expression 'touch wood', for luck, comes from. You would be even luckier if you touched wood from the tree assigned to your Celtic birth month! You can find your tree in Helena Paterson's book: The Celtic Lunar Zodiac – How to Interpret Your Moon Sign *(Rider, 1992).*

The folkloric beliefs and references to trees are vast. From Somerset comes an old rhyme about the nature of certain trees:

> Ellum do grieve
> Oak he do hate
> Willow do walk
> If you travels late.
> Katherine Briggs, *A Book of Fairies* (Penguin Books, 1977), p.30

This meant that if you cut or harmed an elm tree, all the other elms around it would die of grief. Damage or fell an oak and you were in serious trouble, for the oak's spirit would seek revenge and do harm to the guilty person. Perhaps the tree curse to be most feared was that of the willow, as the belief was that to hurt the willow would result in other willow trees following you in the dark – a very scary prospect in times before street lights and torches.

The Elder tree was renowned for housing the spirit of a witch, or powerful mother figure, and the rowan tree for protecting you and your property from harm and evil.

7

SAVING THE FOREST

(SCOTLAND)

Once upon a time, a very long time ago, Scotland was ruled by two goddesses: Bride and Beara. Although they were sisters, they couldn't have been more different. Bride had long blonde hair and bronze, sun-kissed skin. She smiled wherever she went. When Bride ruled the land, all the people were happy.

Beara was as ugly as her sister was beautiful. Her skin was mottled blue, her hair a tangled snarl of purple, and her one eye, which was set in the middle of her forehead, glowed red. When Beara ruled, weather turned foul. Sleet and snow trailed after her and howling winds twined about her knobbly legs. When she arrived, people hid inside their wooden houses, food was scarce and faces were long and drawn.

Back then, most of Scotland was covered in trees, which the people depended upon for food, shelter and heat. They collected nuts and fruit from the woods to feed themselves and their animals. They cut down trees to build their simple round houses. They hunted the deer that lived in the woods for food and in the winter they collected branches off the forest floor to make fires to warm their homes and cook their meals.

When Bride ruled, the trees unfurled their leaves, blossoms bloomed and fruit ripened. The deer grew plump and food was plentiful. The people loved Bride for her generosity. They sang and danced her praises. They never celebrated when Beara was around and as the years passed Beara's jealousy of her sister grew.

Beara and Bride had an agreement: when one was ruling, the other had to stay on an island far to the west. One summer's day, as Beara sat in her island exile gazing into her scrying pool, watching morosely as the people of Scotland held yet another party in honour of her sister, she had an idea. She was not allowed to go to Scotland until Bride's turn was over, but there was no rule against sending someone else over there in her stead. And she had just the perfect someone in mind.

Beara summoned a ferocious dragon to the island. She whispered her plan into his huge golden ear. Then she conjured up an enormous cloud and hid him in the middle of it. She watched eagerly as dragon and cloud flew swiftly towards Scotland.

As the huge, dark cloud settled over the land, blocking out the sun, people stopped smiling. As giant balls of fire began to fall from the cloud, setting alight everything they hit, people ran to hide in their houses.

The fire burned down pine trees, destroyed fruit bushes and nut trees, and chased away the deer. Slowly, but certainly, Scotland's beautiful forest was being destroyed. What were the people to do? The cloud showed no sign of moving.

The king called all his best hunters and warriors to a meeting. 'There is a dragon in that cloud,' he told them, 'and our beloved forest is not safe until the beast is slain.'

The warriors threw their spears into the cloud, but they couldn't see the dragon hidden inside, so their weapons missed their mark. The archers shot their arrows into the cloud, but they too failed to hit their mark and fire continued to fall from the sky.

The people began to despair. There was no more dancing. There was no more singing. Their faces were long with worry. The King called a meeting of all the wisest men and women from across the land. They talked for days, but not one of them could tell him how to get rid of the dragon.

All the while, fire rained down, burning up everything in its path, and the people feared there would be no trees left.

A young girl approached the castle and asked to meet with the King. She claimed she knew how to get rid of the dragon. The guards laughed at her. How could a young girl solve a problem that baffled their wisest elders and fiercest warriors? But they let her through.

The girl's stomach churned as she entered the hall and everyone's eyes turned towards her, but the king smiled kindly and waved her forward. She whispered her plan in his ear. The king nodded thoughtfully, and then he smiled.

He sent his best archers and warriors to the tops of the highest hills. Then he sent messengers to every corner of the Kingdom, ordering people to take the baby animals away from their mothers. They were to take the lambs from the ewes, the foals from the mares, the calves from the cows, the kids from the nanny goats, the chicks from the hens, and the ducklings from the ducks. Even human babies were to be taken away from their human mothers.

As the babies were taken from their mothers, what do you think happened?

They began to cry. Lambs and kids bleated, foals neighed, chicks peeped, calves mooed, ducklings quacked and babies wailed.

High up in the sky, hidden inside the cloud, the dragon heard the growing din. He considered himself to be the most terrifying beast in the world. Yet, in all his long days of murdering and destroying, he had never managed to make anyone sound as miserable as the creatures of this land sounded.

As he listened to the cries, the dragon began to feel afraid. He began to imagine that there must be something larger, more ferocious, and more terrifying than himself down below. He couldn't think of any other reason why everyone would be making such a fuss. What if that terrifying something came after him? If only he could see what was down there. But he couldn't see through the cloud to the ground below any better than the people down there could see him.

Slowly, cautiously, the dragon swooped towards the bottom of the cloud. Slowly, cautiously he stuck his head out of the cloud. He couldn't see anything terrifying, but still the wailing continued. He slipped out a bit further …

As soon as the dragon's chest was visible, the warriors hurled their spears and the hunters loosed their arrows. The weapons found their mark and the dragon fell to the ground. As the cloud melted away, people emerged from their houses and began to smile, to sing and to dance again. Their precious forest had been saved.

NOTES: Many cultures have myths about the struggle between a summer god or goddess and a winter one. This particular version comes from Scotland and features two aspects of the Cailleach, a mother-goddess figure found in Scotland and Ireland. Usually Bride (or Brigit) is the maiden version of the Cailleach and Beara her crone aspect. However, in this story, Bride and Beara are sisters competing over who gets to rule the land.

Involve the audience in telling this story by asking them to identify other animals that might have lived in Scotland many hundreds of years ago. Get them to tell you the names we have for the offspring and the mothers of those species. You can also enroll their help in making sound effects. Have everyone in the audience choose an animal to be and then when the baby animals are separated from the mother animals, have audience members make the noise their animal would make when he or she was upset or scared.

This story speaks of seasons out of balance and makes a good introduction to a discussion of climate change. The forest fires can be used to discuss the extreme weather events that are already taking place around the world. That a young girl comes up with the solution relates to the legacy of problems the older generations are leaving to the younger ones, which the world hopes they will solve.

8

ST MUNGO
AND THE ROBIN

(SCOTLAND, IRELAND)

Many hundreds of years ago, when Christianity was new to Scotland, there lived a great man, named St Serf. It happened one day that St Serf was out walking along the banks of a wide river when he spied a coracle bobbing on the waves. A young woman, clutching a baby to her chest, struggled to paddle the boat to shore. Seeing the woman's distress, St Serf waded into the river, grabbed hold of the gunwale of the boat and pulled it safely up onto the pebbly beach.

The woman was the daughter of King Loth. Her father had banished her for having a baby out of wedlock. St Serf took her and her baby in, nicknaming the boy Mungo, which means 'dear one'.

When he was old enough, Mungo was enrolled at St Serf's school. Mungo proved to be an excellent student. Whatever task St Serf set for his students, Mungo always did it best. He was the quickest to learn the lessons their master set and he never made an error when he recited them back in class. He excelled at solving problems, untangling every one St Serf gave to them and he sang the clearest in choir, his sweet voice always in perfect pitch. St Serf loved him. His classmates did not.

The other boys were jealous of Mungo and did everything they could to make his life miserable. While he recited lessons, they made faces at him behind St Serf's back, trying to distract him. But it never seemed to make a difference; he always had the correct answer on the tip of his tongue. So they gave that up.

They teased him, calling him names, playing tricks on him, trying to get him to lose his temper. But he was too calm and good-natured to get mad at them. So they gave that up.

They tried to entice him into making mischief, but he loved St Serf too much to do anything that would upset him. So they gave that up too.

The boys spent all of their spare time trying to figure out how to get Mungo into trouble. Days turned into weeks, they neglected their homework, got into trouble themselves. Until, finally, one of them had an idea. It involved fire.

In those days, making a fire was long and tedious work. First you had to spin a stick really quickly against a piece of wood, until the friction created a spark of heat. You had to catch that spark on a piece of tinder – moss or dried grass. Then blow on that tinder, hoping it would be dry enough to catch. When it did catch, the flame had to be coaxed into setting bigger branches alight and then those had to set fire to a log. In the depths of winter, when all was damp, making a fire could take ages.

To avoid all the bother, a fire was kept lit day and night in the school's great fireplace. The boys had to take turns tending it. If it went out during the night, the next morning there would be no fire to cook their breakfast porridge, to warm the hall where they studied, or to light the candles for the morning service. If a boy let the fire go out, St Serf would be very angry indeed.

It was Mungo's turn to wake at midnight and feed the fire. As the chapel bell chimed twelve, he got out of his warm bed and padded down to the Great Hall. Before he even entered the room, he knew something was wrong. The air was damp and chill. No glow lit his way. He grabbed a fresh log from the corner and walked towards the fireplace. There was nothing in it but cold white ash and a half-burnt log. The ash had clumped together, as if someone had poured a jug of water on it. The log looked damp too. But Mungo knew he would be the one blamed for being careless, even though he suspected the other boys of playing a trick on him.

Mungo looked at the dry log he held in his hands. If only he could get the fire lit again. He lay the fresh log on the damp ash and blew on it. Nothing happened. He would have to go outside and get some kindling.

Shivering in his nightshirt, Mungo unlocked and opened the huge oak door of the school. Still in his bare feet, he ran across the frost-hardened ground to the nearest tree, which happened to be a hazel. He twisted off a small branch. It burst into flame. Startled, Mungo almost dropped the burning branch, but he managed to hold on tight.

He scurried back inside and dropped the branch in the great hearth. The logs caught fire immediately. Mungo sprang back just in time to avoid being singed. He built up the fire until it was bright and crackling with life, then he tiptoed back to bed.

The next morning, every single boy was out of bed, dressed, face washed, before the morning bell. They had planned their story, practised their lies. They would all pledge that they had left the fire burning when they had gone to bed. Grinning wickedly at each other, anticipating the trouble that Mungo would be in, they pushed and jostled in their hurry to be the first into the Great Hall. When they saw the cheerful fire waiting for them, they stopped and stared. Mungo passed them on his way to the chapel, carrying a lit taper with which to light the candles for morning service.

In that moment, the boys hated Mungo more than ever before.

St Serf loved all of nature's creatures. He had a little robin that'd been orphaned as a nestling that would eat breadcrumbs out of his hand. The little black-eyed robin went everywhere with him, even perching on his shoulder when St Serf sang in the church, warbling along to the hymns. St Serf loved that robin almost as much as he loved Mungo.

One morning, the boys lured the robin into the courtyard with some crumbs. They made sure no one was looking and then they pounced on the poor bird, killed him and pulled his head off. Wailing and crying, they carried the dead bird to St Serf.

'Look what Mungo has done,' they cried. 'Have you ever met such a cruel boy?' A couple of the boys swore to St Serf that they had actually seen Mungo kill the bird.

St Serf went in search of Mungo, the boys trailing after him. They found Mungo, with his nose in a book, studying his lessons. He looked up curiously to see St Serf coming towards him, carrying a small bundle, the other boys trailing behind him, smirking.

As St Serf drew nearer, Mungo realised that the bundle in his hands was a dead robin. 'Oh, no!' he exclaimed.

'Oh no, indeed,' said St Serf. 'I loved this robin as much as I loved you, and look how you have repaid me. What punishment can possibly match such a cruel, hideous act?'

Mungo's cheeks grew red. To be accused unfairly of such a horrible deed was too much even for his good nature. 'I did not touch that robin,' said Mungo. 'I loved that bird as much as you did.'

'You did kill it,' said one of the boys. 'I saw you.'

'I saw you too,' piped another one.

Mungo turned to St Serf. 'I swear, I did not hurt your robin. How can you believe these lies?'

St Serf wanted to believe Mungo, but with all the other boys telling a different story, he couldn't. 'Mungo, if you are innocent, you must prove it,' he said.

Mungo took the robin gently from his teacher's hands. With tears in his eyes, he placed the bird's head back on his shoulders. A fat tear rolled down his face and landed on the bird's severed neck. This was followed by another and another. As Mungo wept and his tears fell on the dead bird, its head became one with its body once more. The feathers on his breast ruffled, as if touched by an unseen wind. He opened his shiny black eyes and gazed up at Mungo, opened his beak and chirped. Mungo gasped in joy, carefully setting the bird back on his feet. The robin fluttered his wings and flew over to land on St Serf's shoulder, where he immediately began to sing.

The other boys slapped their hands over their ears, crying out in pain. But to Mungo the song sounded more beautiful than any music he had ever heard. This time he wept for joy.

St Serf never doubted Mungo's word again and the lying boys were severely punished. With St Serf's help, Mungo went on to do many more brave and fantastic things, becoming himself a saint later in life. But he never forgot the robin, and to the end of his wee life, the robin never forgot Mungo, saving his most beautiful songs for him.

NOTES: St Mungo and his exploits are still celebrated today on the coat of arms for the City of Glasgow, which is accompanied by the following rhyme: 'There's the tree that never grew; There's the bird that never flew; There's the fish that never swam; There's the bell than never rang.'

One pathway to coming to care for a species as a whole or even an entire ecosystem is through coming to care for an individual of that species, such as St Serf's robin. This story can introduce a discussion about caring for wildlife and what to do if you find an injured bird locally.

The other element in this story is fire and heating. We tend to take indoor warmth for granted these days. All we have to do is switch on the central heating. However, as this story demonstrates, lighting a fire and keeping it going used to be much more difficult. This story can introduce a discussion of heating sources, renewables and the importance of insulation. How can we keep the fires burning without hurting the other creatures that dwell on the earth with us?

WATER

9

THE SELKIE BRIDE

(SCOTLAND)

Near the Ayrshire village of Ballantrae, a young fisherman lived in a whitewashed cottage, on the Carrick coast. He took his little boat out every day and brought home a catch of fish to sell at the local pier. It was a good business. Fish merchants bought them and took them to Ayr town where they were sold at the harbour to all the fancy hotels and restaurants.

One evening, as he moored his boat, he spotted a seal lying further out in the bay, on the rocks. The creature was singing its haunting sea song. Fascinated by the seal's gentle sounds, the lad walked quietly over to get a better look. To his surprise, as he came closer he could see this was no ordinary seal. It was a seal-woman washing her hair in a rock pool, her sealskin lying next to her. The amber glow of the setting sun made her skin shimmer with rose and bronze radiance. Her long brown hair caught golden sunbeams, sparkling around her like a halo. The fisherman was entranced by her beauty.

He knew from the tales of selkies and sea-witches told amongst the old fisher-folk, that if he wanted to meet and get a chance to speak with her, then he must take her sealskin away first, or she would disappear under the water forever.

He waded soundlessly through the last stretch of water up to the rock she was sitting on and grabbed up her furry coat. With this hidden under his arm, he touched her shoulder. The seal woman turned and squealed in fright. She looked desperately for her skin, but the young man kept it out of her view. As he gazed into her soft brown eyes, he gasped, stunned by her beauty.

Quite simply, it was love at first sight. With a trembling voice, he declared his love and asked her to marry him. The seal-woman saw how handsome he was, his eyes shone with honesty and love, and what could she do without her sealskin anyway? She blushed and agreed to be his wife.

Together, they lived in his cottage by the sea, happily enjoying each other's company. His love for her grew stronger every day and she appreciated her husband's kindness and thoughtfulness. Sometimes she heard her seal-kin and saw their round, dark heads in the sea, and she longed to know how they all were, but she was contented with her new life, and loved her human well enough.

Until, one morning, she woke from a dream that had disturbed her; she'd dreamed that her sealskin was above the boards, in the roof rafters. All day long, she kept busy with the household chores, trying her best to ignore the thought of her seal-fur being up in the roof. The following night and the next, the same dream of her hidden skin came back to her. By the third morning she was desperate to find out if the dream was true.

As soon as her man went out in his boat, she stood on a stool and felt about in the rafters. Her hand touched soft fur and a shudder of recognition went through her. Fetching it down, she couldn't resist pulling the thick warm, familiar coat over her shoulders. She was over-come with the urge to go to the sea.

As if the tidal pull was drawing her also, she found herself running to the waters' edge, wrapped tightly in her old sealskin. The cries of gulls and the sound of waves rhythmically breaking onto rocks filled her ears. Her toes touched the cold salt water and the smell of seaweed engulfed her senses. She slipped effortlessly into the waves. On she swam to find her seal family, deeper and deeper into the dark green sea she plunged, her seal body racing through the water.

The fisherman arrived home that night to an empty cottage. He saw the stool under the open ceiling boards, and knew instantly that he'd lost his beautiful selkie wife back to the sea and the seals. All night he walked up and down the coast, calling her name and listening to the sound of seals singing a song of joy far out at sea.

For a month the heartbroken husband walked day and night, calling out to his lost wife along the beaches of the Carrick shore. On the last Sunday of the month, he stumbled upon an empty seal-fur draped over a rock. Putting it on, he felt an unstoppable urge to swim in the clear green water. Down he plunged into the depths, to the land where his wife and her seal-kin lived.

The gentle seals accepted their new son-in-law with kindness. When he and his sweetheart were reunited, she felt the overwhelming love he had for her and agreed to come back up onto land and live as a human again.

They enjoyed life together above the sea, and as the years rolled on, their house was filled with their bonnie children. Bringing up the family kept them busy and the selkie-woman had little time to think of her other family below the waves. But one night the dream of her sealskin came back to her. Three nights in a row, she dreamed of swimming in her seal-coat, deep beneath the waters. This time she found her fur in the thatch. The same compelling need to be in the water pulled her back to the sea. She knew that her love for her man and children was the greatest in her life, but she could not deny the overwhelming longing of her soul to be with the seals. She swam again, back into the sea as her real self, a seal.

Her husband searched for her each day and night. He was rewarded. Every Sunday for six weeks, he found a new empty sealskin left on the rocks: one for him and each of their five children.

When the fisherman and four of his bairns could wait no longer to be reunited with their seal-mother, they put on their skins and joined her in the mer-country of the seals. The oldest son, however, had left home some time before to look for work on the land. He had never wanted to be a fisherman. Instead, he had found a job on a farm in the hills behind Ballantrae. Here was his heart's desire: ploughing and sowing the dark, earthy soil, waiting to reap the rich golden harvest of corn from the land. From this farm, he could see the sealskin left on the rocks for him. He watched the tides come up and wash over it, the sun bleach it, and the wind tatter it, until one day it floated away in ragged pieces. Only then did he feel free of his ties to his family and the sea. Now, his own independent life as a farmer could truly begin.

Soon enough he married his sweetheart, a dairy-maid, and together they had a family of their own. Often he would tell them stories of their seal grandparents and aunts and uncles. Of course they never believed his stories and laughed merrily at the idea of having seal relations. But he kept a special eye on all of his children whenever they played on the beach close to the rocks, where their seal-cousins frolicked in the salty foam.

NOTES: A happy ending that highlights a families' resilience and ability to change. While the seal mother must return to her element of water, most of her human family give up their familiar way of life to be with her. The one boy, who stays to become a farmer, perhaps gives us the strongest message in the story – follow your own path. You do not have to do what your parents have done before you. Change is possible.

10

THE TIDDY MUN

(ENGLAND)

Long ago, the boggy marshland of the Cars in England was home to more ghosts, spirits and strange creatures than anyone could dare to name. There were boggarts, will-o' the-wisps, body-less voices, hands without arms, todlowries and witches who rode on great, black water snakes. All these ghosties and ghoulies came out at night and scared people nearly to death.

There was only one wetland spirit whom folk could trust, and that was the Tiddy Mun. He lived deep down in the green water holes, only coming out at night when the mists rose. He was just a tiny, wee man – the size of a three-year-old child, and that's why he was called 'Tiddy Mun'. He would creep from his watery home and limp along the roads. His hair and beard were long, tangled and white; he looked like a tiny, old grandfather. He wore a long grey cloak, so you could barely see him in the mist, just a shimmer of eerie shadow. But folk heard him as he whistled in tune with the wind, and sometimes he laughed loudly and clearly like the peewit bird.

Tiddy Mun was not an evil spirit like the rest of the ghouls in the Cars; he helped the local people and they respected him. During the rainy, wet months, if the water level was rising high and coming too near their homes, the whole family would go out into the night and ask for his help. They would call out loud, 'Tiddy Mun wi'out a name, tha watter's thruff!'

They would chant this verse until they heard the call of the peewit across the marsh. Then they knew he had heard them and they could go home.

The next morning, the waters would have gone down and the people's homes would be saved from flooding.

Sadly though, everything changed when the Dutchmen were hired to drain the wetlands. The men arrived to do the drainage work and the people were promised great benefit and riches. They said that draining the wild, wet, boggy land was progress. But the farmers and local folk knew that no good would come of it, because where would the 'ole granfer' live if his water pools were dried up?

Many Dutchmen disappeared mysteriously into the mists, never to be seen again. The Car-folk spoke of the Tiddy Mun; they knew he was growing angrier, and that he was the one responsible for the men vanishing.

The authorities just sent for more men from Holland to drain the water from the land. As the Cars grew drier and drier – the water flowing away in ditches to the rivers – the Tiddy Mun eventually lost his patience with the Car-folk, as well as the Dutchies. Tiddy made the cattle ill, he curdled the cow's milk, babies became very sick with a strange fever and many died, and all the crops in the fields perished. The people were starving and dying.

At first they blamed the wicked bogles and witches. Many poor old herb-wives and men gifted with prophecy were accused of witchcraft. They suffered terribly, before being put to death by the desperate and ignorant townsfolk. But still the harvests failed and illness plagued the community and their livestock. Finally, they realised that it must be their old ally the Tiddy Mun who was sending bad luck and pestilence their way.

The whole community came together to plan a way to let the Tiddy Mun know that they could not stop the draining of the land; that they too wanted none of this so-called progress. Each man, woman and child took a bowl or cup of water and gathered at the dyke.

Each poured their water out carefully and they all called, 'Tiddy Mun wi'out a name, here's watter for thee, tak tha spell undone.'

At first all was eerie silence, then the sound of crying, wailing children could be heard rising up all around them. The pitiful cries grew louder, as the unseen spirits drew closer. Tiny, invisible hands reached out for the women and cold babies' lips kissed the mothers. The women said it was the infants they had lost to illness. The children's spirits were calling to the Tiddy Mun to forgive them, lift the spell and help their families. Silence followed as the night darkened. Then the cry of the peewit echoed out, across the land.

The Cars-folk sighed with relief, for they knew the Tiddy Mun was lifting the curse of bad luck. The Tiddy Mun was still their friend, the good, little grandfather. Some cheered for joy, some grieved for the spirits of their lost babies, but all went home with new hope and light hearts.

From that time onwards, the curse was lifted and the people prospered. Families remembered to go out together on the new moon and pour cups of water into the dyke, as a peace offering and sign of respect to the Tiddy Mun. Those who didn't observe this ritual grew sick and died.

But over many years, the community forgot about the Tiddy Mun. As new generations were born, the old ways no longer seemed important and the little old grandfather was abandoned on the moors. Maybe he is gone now, or maybe he still hides away in deep watery places, whistling in the wind and laughing with the peewit.

NOTES: This haunting tale about the forgotten spirits of the land is a reminder about what is lost when habitats are improved, drained and changed for human use. The ecological balance is disturbed and altered. This is a good introduction to discussions about wetland habitats and the need for biodiversity. It also highlights the need for community cohesion over the stewardship of the environment. When these wetland areas were drained, old spirits and old beliefs faded away. This poignant folk legend reminds us of the richness of a diverse landscape, with many types of habitat and spirits.

11

THE SUNKEN PALACE

(IRELAND)

Once upon a time, in a valley far in the south of Ireland, there was a king who was blessed by having a well that was filled with the clearest, sweetest water anyone had ever tasted. So sweet was this water that he built his whole castle around it. So sweet was this water that he named his first and only child Fior Usga (Spring Water) in honour of the well. So sweet was this water that everyone came from miles around to fill their drinking vessels. The rich and the poor, the young and the old, the brooding and the joyful, all came to the king's courtyard to quench their thirst at his well.

This did not please the king. It was tiresome to have people constantly knocking at his gate, clamouring to fill their jugs and water skins, their goblets and barrels, their jars and their flagons with the clear, sweet water. After all it was his well, in his courtyard, enclosed by the tall walls and ramparts of his castle! What good was it to be king, if he was to be constantly surrounded by crowds of subjects?

His daughter enjoyed the crowds. When the king complained about the constant queues of people littering up his courtyard, she shrugged. No matter how much water was drawn, the well never ran dry. In fact, the water always seemed sweeter on days when many people had come to draw up the bucket. And everyone was so grateful, stopping to thank her if she happened to be crossing from the Great Hall to the kitchens, which she made sure to do many times a day when crowds had gathered. It made her feel important and happy to be thanked by them.

One day, it took the king an entire hour to cross from one side of the courtyard to the other, because there were so many people wanting to tell him how generous and kind he was. When he finally reached the Great Hall, he sent for his stonemason and instructed him to build a high wall around the well and to fit it with a thick oak door, guarded by a heavy, iron lock.

The king had two golden keys made to fit the lock. One he kept on a chain around his neck, the other he gave to his steward, whom he trusted above everyone else.

Now when people came to the castle carrying their flagons and jugs, their water skins and barrels, they were turned away. 'The water belongs to the King,' said the guard at the gate, 'and he has decreed that it be kept exclusively for his household's use.'

Now when the princess crossed the empty courtyard, there was no one to thank her, to bless her, to ask after her father's health. The sound of her footsteps echoed hollowly off the wall that enclosed the well. Soon she stopped crossing the courtyard. Then she stopped leaving her room. Some days she didn't even bother to get out of bed.

The king worried about his one and only child, his Fior Usig, his Clear Water. He announced that he would hold a ball in her honour. He'd heard that princesses like balls, and it seemed to work. The very next day, she sprang out of bed early in the morning to begin writing invitations.

On the night of the ball, the princess was radiant, smiling and greeting each new arrival. Several charming young men had accepted her invitation, including a prince or two. Once the music started, she was kept busy dancing with them. One particularly handsome prince caught her fancy. He was dashing and graceful. When she was in his arms, her feet scarcely touched the floor. She danced with him more than once.

And then there was the feast. The wooden tables creaked and groaned with the weight of all the food. It was more than the whole company would be able to eat, even if they stayed an entire fortnight. But there was no water.

The princess led the handsome prince to the high table to meet her father. The king asked him if he was enjoying the ball.

'The company is delightful,' he said, smiling at the princess, 'the food is delectable, but with all this dancing, my thirst is great. I would love a taste of the clear, sweet water that your castle is renowned for.'

This was the moment the king had been waiting for. While his daughter had been planning the ball, he had been conspiring with his goldsmith, who had created a water jug made of pure gold.

'My daughter will fetch you some of my clear, sweet water,' said the king, clapping his hands. The steward stepped forward carrying the gold jug and the gold key. The crowd exclaimed at the beauty of the jug, but the princess frowned. She did not like being ordered about like a common serving girl.

Her beloved prince, sensing her displeasure, bowed to the king. 'Kind sir, it would be my honour to escort your daughter on this important errand.'

'Suit yourself,' said the king, dismissing the pair with a wave of his hand, wondering how much this prince's kingdom might be worth.

The princess felt quite breathless as she led the handsome prince through the Great Hall and out into the moonlit courtyard. She fumbled with the golden key. The prince took it gently from her hand and turned it easily in the lock. The door swung open and he followed her inside.

The princess looked down into the well. It was the first time she had been near it in over a year. The water was lower than she remembered, almost out of reach. She lowered the golden jug towards the water, but it seemed to pull away from her. Not wanting to disappoint the prince, she leaned even further over the rim of the well, the golden jug heavy and awkward in her grasp. Still she could not reach. She stood up on her tiptoes and stretched her arms as far as they would reach, and lost her balance. She fell, tumbling headlong into the well, still clutching the golden jug.

The prince shouted, lunging after her, holding out his hand. But he was too late. She disappeared beneath the surface of water, which was now rising at an alarming speed. He tried to reach for her under the water, but the force of it gushing up out of the ground pushed him back. It spilled out of the well and washed him out into the courtyard.

He sprang to his feet and ran towards the Great Hall, hoping to warn the king and his guests, but the water got there first. In a matter of minutes, the entire castle was submerged.

The next morning, the sun rose over a new lake, where once a valley had been. On a clear day, it is still possible to see the castle, deep under the water, and all the guests still dancing and eating. The princess is there too, with her prince.

Now anyone can go down to the shore of the lake and enjoy the sweet, clear water that the king tried so hard to keep for himself.

NOTES: There are many tales around the British Isles about sunken villages and castles. These legends are usually connected to specific lakes, lochs and inlets. In some of these places there are the remains of old habitations, submerged through natural means or by intentional damming.

Clean drinking water for people and clean, habitable water for marine and freshwater species is at risk due to droughts, flooding, pollution and overfishing. This story tells of nature's revenge when one person tries to prevent others from having access to a resource that should be held in common.

12

SEAL ISLAND

(SCOTLAND, TRAVELLER)

There was once a crofter who lived happily with his wife and five sons, on their fine big croft in Argyll. The chap spent one or two days a week fishing in his boat and the rest of the time working the land. But as his sons grew older, he knew that there wasn't enough work for all of them on a single croft. So, one evening after dinner, he and his wife called a meeting of the whole family. They sat around the big kitchen table and discussed their options for the future. They were worried that one or two of them might have to go and find work away from the family, but none of them had the heart for this. Eventually, after much talk, they decided that the two oldest boys could work the croft with their father, and the three youngest ones could take the boat and make a living from fishing. They were happy with this new arrangement, it meant they could all live at home and continue to enjoy their good life together and their mother's fine cooking.

The new arrangement began well enough, with the older boys doing much of the farming –they reared the cattle, tended the sheep flock, ploughed with the horses and grew crops. Their father was getting older, so he left the heavy physical work to his two fine strapping lads and concentrated on his chickens, ducks, geese and dogs. Mother had her vegetable garden and six hungry men to feed, so everyone was busy about the house and land.

The three younger sons took their father's boat and started their new careers as fishermen. Now, fishing was very good back then. The shoals of cod, mackerel and herring were plentiful, and there were far fewer people in the world to feed. The boys did well for the first few months, catching plenty of fish, which they took to the local pier and sold on to market. Many crofters had boats and the fish were sold up and down the whole coastline; it was a thriving business.

The brothers took their boat out each day to the sea-loch, but as the weather changed with the seasons, they began to find it too rough to fish there, and had to go further, past a wee rocky island about two miles out from the loch. The waters were calmer here and they caught big netful's of fish around the island. Every now and then, the seals would find the nets and help themselves to a fish or two, leaving a half-eaten one behind. This annoyed the three brothers – a half-eaten fish was no good to them, and they would have to throw the remains back into the water. Each time they found the head and tail of a cod, or a mackerel eaten clean in two, they would grumble to each other and curse the seals for stealing their catch.

One evening, their father asked them how the fishing was going. The boys gave their mother money for the housekeeping each month – some of their earnings from their fish sales – but he'd noticed they hadn't given her any this month.

'Well father, it's been fine up 'til this last wee while,' said the oldest of the three, he was nineteen years old.

'It's those damn seals!' the youngest boy grumbled.

'Yes father it's true. They're eating more and more of the fish we catch,' the middle boy added.

The oldest of the three kept on moaning about the seals, while his father listened silently.

'It's not even that they eat a whole fish father. They eat a fish in half and leave the rest to rot.'

'And tear our nets into the bargain!' protested the youngest son.

All three boys grew red in the face with anger as they complained about the seals.

When they had finished, their father spoke quietly, but firmly, 'Now listen carefully, the three of you. I've fished the waters around here for longer than you've lived. That island is Seal Island. That's where the seal-people live and raise their young. They need the fish too you know! And they have as much right to those fish as any of us. The seal people are my friends and you had better leave them in peace and stay away from their island.'

The boys knew their father had a soft spot for the creatures. They thought it was very odd the way he called the seals, 'people'. They decided not to mention the seals to their father again; best not to upset him like this. But they kept fishing the abundant waters around that small, uninhabited island, even though he'd told them to stay away. And the seals carried on tearing their nets and eating the fish. The younger sons resented this bitterly and grumbled and moaned about it amongst themselves daily.

Eventually, they decided to do something about the seals, to put a stop to their fish stealing. They planned to go out to the island at about six or seven in the evening. This was when the seals all came onto the rocks to bask in the late sun. Then the boys would club the little ones and stone the bigger ones to death and be rid of the whole lot of them once and for all.

After dinner the next evening, the three youngest boys got up, mumbled something about mending nets and checking the boat and went out. Their brothers were deep into newspapers and books, their father was nodding off to sleep in his chair by the fire, and their mother was busy, as usual, in the kitchen – no one paid the three lads any notice whatsoever.

They collected wooden clubs from the woodshed and rowed out to Seal Island.

When they arrived, there were no seals to be seen anywhere. This was very strange.

'They must be out chasing fish late tonight,' said the oldest. 'We'll get onto land and wait for them.'

'Aye, two miles is a fair way to row, so I'm for waiting a while too,' the second brother agreed, his arms tired.

The youngest lad, who was only sixteen, was happy to do what his brothers told him. They rowed up the tiny inlet to a rocky cove with a small beach and landed their boat in the sheltered bay. From the sea, this was the only way onto the island. Here they were surrounded by the high cliffs they had climbed in search of gull's eggs when they were younger. Driftwood had collected at the waters' edge.

'We'll have a fire here, and wait for the seals to arrive.'

The middle boy moored the boat, while the others collected wood and made a fire.

'It's awful queer though,' the oldest mused, 'there's usually a hundred or more of the creatures around here at this time, all lazing about the rocks.'

The brothers sat around their fire in the sheltered bay for a while. They smoked and went over their plan some more. Suddenly, the youngest lad sat up straight and turned to look behind him. 'What's that I hear?'

'It'll be the seals coming in for the night. Get ready boys.' His older brother replied.

'No, I hear voices … human voices!' The young lad strained his ears.

The brothers were puzzled. No one ever came to the island – well, very rarely. There was so little access; only seals and birds lived here.

A person came into view, walking up over the rocks and stepping onto the grass. He was tall and broad, a mature man with greying hair. Behind this man, many more people appeared, a whole tribe of them walking onto the beach. They surrounded the boys and their fire.

The brothers' jaws fell open – where had this colony of people come from? There must have been one hundred and fifty folk standing about them – old men and women, young ones, children, teens, toddlers and mothers carrying babies.

They were talking amongst themselves in a strangely accented mixture of Gaelic and English. But what puzzled the brothers most was the way these people were dressed – they were all wearing strange, brown furry coats and leggings, and some had hats and mittens made of thick, brown pelt.

The large, grey haired man stepped forward and spoke directly to the three brothers, 'We know why you came here tonight. You came to club our children to death and to smash the skulls of our mothers and fathers, brothers and sisters with rocks and stones. You came here to murder us.'

The three lads jumped to their feet, shocked and frightened. The strangers were talking and muttering, 'That's them. Aye they're the ones, as would kill us wi' clubs and stones.'

The eldest boy spoke, 'Excuse me sir, but we did not come here to kill you. We came here to kill the seals that steal our fish. We've never seen you before in our lives – who are you?'

The large man spoke, 'We are the seal-people. This is our island and our fish. We are the seals you came here to kill. The elders and I have had a meeting and agreed that we will do exactly to you, what you had planned to do to us.'

The lads noticed that each of the seal-people had a club or rock in their hands. The three young men were terrified. The seal-folk were between them and their boat; there was no way to escape other than up the cliff.

'Please,' begged the eldest lad, 'we didn't know that you were anything more than animals …'

An old, croaky voice shouted out from the beach, 'Wait a minute now! Stop a moment kinfolk! Here, let me through.' An elderly, white-haired man, small with age, pushed carefully through the crowd, stepping right up to the tall leader.

'What is it grandfather?' The large seal-man asked kindly.

'Friends and family, you must stop this. Just wait a minute and let me speak.' The old man smiled around at his kinsmen and women and they stopped talking to listen to him.

'I missed the elders meeting earlier. I was away collecting driftwood!' The old man waved the fine plank of sea-bleached oak-wood that he had in his hands. 'We must spare these foolish boys' lives. I know what they came here to do to us, but let me tell you why we must let them go free …'

The big leader nodded, stepped aside and let his grandfather, in his shabby brown seal-fur coat, step forward to speak.

'When I was a young seal, just a pup learning to hunt food for myself, I was caught in their father's net. I'd foolishly put my head and flippers in to bite a fish, and had become completely entangled. I would have died in that net if the boys' father hadn't pulled me out and set me free. So you see kinsfolk, I and many of you, my children and grandchildren and great-grandchildren, wouldn't be here today if their kinsman had not been so good and kind to me. He saved my life and I owe it to him to save his sons' lives too.'

The seal-people murmured and nodded their heads in agreement. The old seal-man turned to the three lads. 'We see the fish you catch in your nets, and they are our fish, here to feed our children. There are many other places, away from here, where you can catch plenty of fish, but this is our home. You must go and fish in other waters.'

The grey-haired man put his hand on his grandfather's shoulder. 'We will do as you wish grandfather. One good turn deserves another.' He turned to the boys and said sternly, 'We will respect grandfather's wishes and let you go, but if you bother us in the future, I cannot promise your safety in these waters.'

The seal-people stood aside, letting the lads return to their boat. The boys rowed as fast as they could all the way to shore, full of fear that the seals might change their minds. When they got back to the house, they went in, looking as white as ghosts and trembling with adrenaline. Their father looked at them curiously.

The oldest of the three broke the silence. 'We went to see if we could land any night fish near seal island father.'

'Oh aye,' the old man replied, 'and did you have any luck?'

'N-no …' the youngest stammered, his voice still shaking.

'No, father,' the eldest said. 'We've decided the waters are too rough there. From now on we'll just leave that place to the … seals.'

'Aye, we'll find new fishing grounds, father,' the middle boy said carefully, 'and leave the island to your seal-folk.'

Their father smiled and nodded. 'Aye lads, there's plenty o' fish in the sea for all of us.'

NOTES: This was a story told to the late storyteller and traveller, Duncan Williamson. Since Duncan met the crofter who told him this story in the late twentieth century, the cod have almost disappeared from the waters around the west coast of Scotland. Ever-growing demand from the human world has left fewer and fewer fish for the creatures that inhabit the sea. This magical story illustrates the need to live in harmony with our fellow creatures, and manage the earth's reserves for everyone, human and animal alike.

EARTH

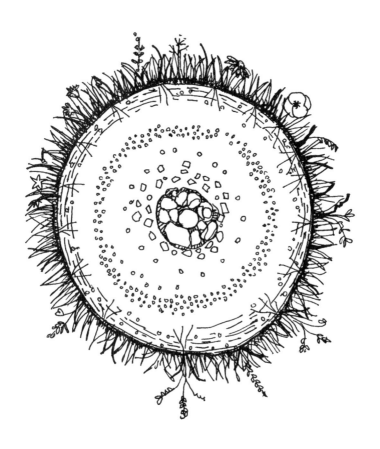

13

THE BLAEBERRY GIRL

(IRELAND)

One summer's day, a young girl was sent by her Gran to pick the blaeberries that were ripening on the bushes on the hillside behind their cottage. The girl took her bucket and ran happily up the hill for it was a fine, sunny day and she loved blaeberries.

She made her way from bush to bush. 'One for the bucket.' Ping, the blaeberry hit the bottom of the bucket. 'And one for me.' She popped a sour sweet berry into her mouth.

'Two for the bucket.' Ping. 'And two for me.' Another sweet sour berry went into her mouth.

'Three for the bucket.' Ping. 'And three for me.' Up and up the hill she went, filling her bucket and filling her belly.

The sun was beating down and her mouth was dry from the sourness of the berries, so when she came to a little bubbling stream, she knelt down, cupped her hand and took a long drink of the cool, clear water. As she leaned over the stream, she heard a jingle of music behind her. She turned around, but there was nothing to be seen.

Once again she leaned over to take a drink. Once again she heard music but when she whirled around, the music disappeared. This girl always listened to her Gran and her Gran was a very wise old woman, so the girl had a fairly good idea what, or I should say 'who', was playing the tune.

She leaned over the stream one more time, but she didn't fill her hands with water. Instead, she waited and listened.

Sure enough, the tune started up again. She reached around behind her back and grabbed at the sound. Something wriggled and squirmed in her fist. Carefully, she turned around and looked at it, or I should say 'him', for it was an ugly wee man with a snaggled, knotted beard. He was wearing a tiny, old-fashioned suit of tweed. It was, in fact, a leprechaun.

'Unhand me, you monster!' shouted the little man. Although his shout was not very loud, as he was small enough to fit in the girl's hand.

As I've said, the girl always listened closely to the stories her Gran told, so she knew that leprechauns always keep a pot of gold buried somewhere nearby. She also knew that leprechauns must always tell the truth, although they can never be trusted.

'I will let you go, if you tell me where your pot of gold is hidden,' said the girl.

The leprechaun tried his best not to speak, he sputtered and pressed his hand against his mouth. His face began to turn a particularly strange sort of bluish-red colour. As I've already told you, leprechauns cannot lie, and that includes lying by not saying anything.

'Over there, under that blaeberry bush,' said the leprechaun, finally, through gritted teeth. 'Now put me down.'

The girl shook her head. 'There are lots of blaeberry bushes over there. You are going to have tell me exactly which one has the pot of gold underneath it.'

She took the leprechaun over to the nearest bush. 'Is your pot of gold buried under this bush?' she asked.

The leprechaun's face turned scarlet. Reluctantly he shook his head.

She carried him to the next bush and asked the same thing. He shook his head again. They went from bush to bush until finally they came to one that was in the middle of the hillside. This time, the leprechaun nodded his head.

Just to be sure, the girl asked him again, 'Is your pot of gold buried under this bush?'

'Yes, yes, yes, yes, yes!' he spluttered angrily. 'Now put me down!'

The girl was about to set his little feet back on the ground when she had a thought. In order to dig up the gold, she would have to fetch a spade from the cottage. 'I will put you down,' she said, 'if you promise not to move your pot of gold.'

By this time, the leprechaun's face was the colour of a boiled beet but he said, 'I promise not to move my pot of gold.'

She had another thought. 'You have to promise not to move the bush either.'

The leprechaun looked at her crossly, but he said 'I promise not to move the bush either. Now let me go. This is most undignified.'

She looked at the bush again. How would she be able to tell which bush it was when she came back? They all looked more or less the same.

'I will put you down, if you take the blue ribbon from around my pony-tail and tie it around the bush.' She held the leprechaun up to her head so he could untie her ribbon. Looking extremely grouchy indeed, he tied the ribbon onto a branch of the bush.

She lowered him towards the ground. 'And you must promise not to untie that ribbon,' she said as his feet touched the ground.

'I promise not to untie the ribbon,' he said.

She released him from her grasp.

Pop! He disappeared.

The girl ran down the hill to fetch the spade, daydreaming all the away about all the nice things she was going to buy with her pot of gold. She'd have so much money she could even pay someone to pick blaeberries for her!

Carrying her shining spade, she walked back up the hill. She hadn't gone far when she saw the bush with her ribbon on it. She dug it up, roots and all. No pot of gold. She dug deeper and deeper. Still nothing!

She paused to stand up and wipe the sweat off her forehead. That's when she noticed that the blaeberry bush next to this one also had a blue ribbon tied to it, and so did the next one, and the next one, and the one after that. In fact, all the blaeberry bushes on the hill had ribbons on them!

But the girl wasn't ready to give up. She dug up first one bush, then another, and then another, until more than half of them were lying with their roots in the air. The girl never did find that pot of gold and the blaeberry bushes? It took them many years to grow back and their berries never did taste as juicy and sour sweet as they did before she met that leprechaun.

NOTES: Blaeberries are found all over the British Isles as well as in Europe, and are variously known as bilberries, whortleberries, whinberries, hurts, myrtle blueberries, and fraughans. They are closely related to North American blueberries. When telling this story, you can invite your audience to pick the berries with you, counting 'one for the bucket, one for me. Two for the bucket, two for me,' and so on.

14

STOLEN BY FAIRIES

(ENGLAND)

Long ago, the Weardale valley, in County Durham, was known to be full of fairies. People said that they lived in the little caves that go back under the hills. On moonlit nights they held their fairy celebrations in these hillside crevices and underground palaces. On rare occasions, men coming back late at night from the pub would see the fairy people dancing by the rocky outcrops. But more often, folk only heard them playing their otherworldly musical instruments, singing and laughing – their melodic voices gurgling in time to the flow of the streams running down the hillside. Sometimes, people coming home through the dale on dark nights disappeared, vanished! Many believed it was the fairies who took them away. The little people were secretive and sometimes spiteful creatures who couldn't stand being seen by humans. Folk who discovered their hiding places could be spirited away – stolen by fairies – gone from the human world for ever.

One spring morning, a farmer's daughter was out playing on the hillside above the farm. She was filling her pockets with pretty wild primroses, when she heard the sound of the fairies celebrating their May-time revels. Curious to see the little folk, she crept around the rocky outcrop. There below, she spied them at the mouth of their cave.

Delighted to see such beautiful creatures playing, dancing and singing, the child clapped her hands in joy and gasped out-loud, 'Oh my, there they are … the merry fairy-folk!'

Immediately the fairies fled back down into their secret dwelling under the hill, angry that a human child had seen them.

The little girl couldn't wait to share this secret with her father and she ran back to the farmhouse to tell him. He listened quietly and carefully as she described the fairies' May-Day dance on the hillside. He didn't show his deep concern after he'd heard her story, instead he carried on as normal, without a word of worry to her. But after supper, when he had tucked his child up in bed and given her a goodnight kiss, the farmer put on his boots and hurried out of the house. He made straight for the wise woman's cottage in the next village.

After he explained the situation to old Sara, she shook her head and said in a serious tone, 'You are right to be worried. Indeed the fairy-folk will not stand for human interference in their private affairs. They will come for your daughter and try and take her away from you tonight, around midnight.'

The farmer pleaded with wise Sara for a charm to protect his dear child.

'Well, you see, they cannot cast their magic and steal your girl away, if there is no noise to disturb their work. So what you must do is go back to your homestead and make sure it is completely silent. Especially when they come at the witching hour; at that time your place must be as quiet as can be – not a sound! If you can do this, your little one will be safe.'

The farmer thanked Sara for her wise words and galloped off through the dark night on his horse. All the way home, he thought about what was in his house that could make noise. As he jumped off his mare, he turned her and his plough horses out of their stables and into a far field – this would keep their hooves from clattering noisily in the stalls. Then he went to his cows' byre and took their chains and halters off, to prevent them clinking and clanging during the night. He bolted the door and went to his dogs, giving them a bucket of milk and basin of fresh meat for their supper. The dogs had never eaten so well in their lives and when they were secure in their kennel, each dog fell fast asleep. Next, he looked to his hen house. He covered the window with old sackcloth, to stop the moon from shining in and disturbing the roosting chickens. Finally, he went to the pigs and dumped as much straw as he could into their sty. Their snorts and grunts were soon well muffled under it. He fed them grain and bolted the door securely.

Then into his house he strode. First, he covered the birdcage with a blanket, so that the parrot would sleep quietly. Next, the kettle came off the hob in case steam should hiss from the spout. He kicked the logs from the fire and poured water over the embers to kill all sparks and crackling in the grate. Then he silenced the clocks in the house. He took off his heavy work boots, and sat in his woolly socks, as quiet as a mouse. He heard the church bells chime midnight in the village and soon the sound of tiny horses hooves came clattering over his yard. It was the fairies on their ponies. Up to his door they raced, but there they paused. They sensed that something was wrong, that there was no sound or movement anywhere about. The farmer held his breath for fear of being heard. Into his home, the fairy folk poured, through the keyholes and letterbox. Up the stairs to his daughter's bedroom they flew to the sound of magical, miniature hooves. Silence everywhere. Then, suddenly, a dog began to bark!

The farmer leaped up the stairs, four at a time, but arrived at his little girl's room too late. Her bed was empty, the fairies and child gone. There, at the foot of the bed was her pet dog, barking for all he was worth. The farmer had completely forgotten that the little terrier slept upstairs with his daughter. The creature's senses had alerted him to the supernatural invasion, but too late to save the lass from the kidnapping. The farmer stayed up all night with an aching heart, wondering what he could do next.

As soon as the sun rose, he saddled his mare and rode back to the wise wife's door. She sat him down and counselled him. 'Only once have I known of anyone returning from the fairy-realm.'

'I would do anything to get my girl back,' the farmer said, tears in his eyes. 'That child is all I have, she means more to me than anything in this world. Please tell me what I am to do.'

Wise Sara spoke kindly to him. 'This is no easy task for you, but if you can go to the exact place where she first saw the little people and give them three special presents, then all will be well. You must wear a sprig of rowan for your own protection. Here is what you must do: Take with you a light which does not burn, a living bird with no bones in its body, and the limb of a creature, taken without shedding any blood. If you can take these three gifts to the fairy king, then you may get your girl back.'

The farmer thanked Sara with all his heart and rode back towards his home, his mind full of puzzlement at how he might find these strange gifts.

An old beggar man lay at the side of the road. He raised a trembling hand towards the farmer as he passed. 'Please sir, can you spare some change for a poor old body, to pay for soup and bread at the village inn?'

The farmer reached inside his jacket, pulled out a sixpence and gave it to the old fella. The beggar man's eyes began to twinkle and he spoke in a stronger voice. 'It's a kind man who would help an old tramp, when that man plainly has worries of his own. For your generosity to me, I will tell you the answer to the first of your riddles; 'tis a glow-worm that gives out light without burning.'

The farmer was amazed, 'Of course! Why hadn't he thought of that?' He began to thank the tramp, but as he opened his mouth to speak, the old man shimmered for a moment and then vanished.

The farmer hurried his horse on; at least he now had the answer to one of the questions.

A thrush flew in front of the horse, landing squawking and flapping in the bushes. There, hovering above it, was a hawk ready to swoop upon the frightened bird. The farmer grabbed a stone from the road and threw it at the bird of prey. The hawk flew away, leaving the thrush to escape unharmed.

The small bird cocked it's head to one side, opened its beak and spoke directly to the farmer, 'A caring, goodly soul you are to save my life, when you have so many woes of your own. For your kindness to me I will give you a gift. The bird with no bones in its body, is a chick of a hen, only fifteen days old, living inside the egg.'

The farmer's jaw dropped in amazement. Why, he had plenty of hens and fertilized eggs at his farm, this riddle was no problem to him now. He thanked the magical bird. As he did so, it chirped and vanished before his eyes.

Once more he set out towards his farm, only stopping to gather three glowworms from the roots of a big old tree, along the way. As he put them safely in his pocket, he noticed a rabbit squealing and kicking in a snare at the edge of the road. He could not stand for this type of cruelty to a living beast, so he bent down and gently released the creature's leg from the harsh, wire trap.

Usually when freed, a rabbit would dash away, but this creature turned to look at the farmer, and spoke. 'Even though you have troubles of your own, you have stopped to help me, so I will repay your kindness and help you. Take the tail of a lizard, for this you can pull from the owner without shedding blood.'

The farmer smiled for joy and began to thank the wild rabbit, but it flickered in the light and disappeared into thin air. He was beginning to get used to all the strange happenings of the day!

Once home, he turned his horse into the field, and went over to the hen house. He looked to his broody hens and counted the days since they'd laid. Sure enough one hen was sitting on an egg, fifteen days old. The farmer took it, wrapped it in a hanky and put it gently into his pocket. Then he climbed the hill. There, on a big rock, sat a lizard, heating itself in the warm sunshine. The farmer crept up behind the snoozing reptile and grabbed its tail ... POP! The lizard sped away in fright, leaving its tail in his hand, and not a drop of blood was spilled. Next he took a sprig of green rowan and tucked it firmly into his cap. Then he set off to the caves where his child had described her first meeting with the fairies.

As the farmer approached the rocks, he bent down on his knees and peered into the dark opening between the boulders. He cleared his throat, as shy men often do before speaking, and called out, 'Fairy-folk, give me back my daughter.'

The fairies heard him and rushed furiously up through their cave towards him. They saw the rowan twig and stopped.

He laid the glow-worms, the fifteen day-old egg, with a live boneless chick inside, and the lizard's tail down in front of them.

'Here are three gifts for your king. Now please may I have my little girl back?' The farmer waited as the fairies snatched up the strange presents.

The king of the fairies inspected the gifts and smiled. He clapped his little hands and the fairies and gifts disappeared. Moments later the farmer's daughter emerged out of the cave and jumped into her father's open arms. He hugged his child for all he was worth. Together they went back to the farmhouse. The two of them sat down to eat toast and tea at the kitchen table. The child told her father what fun it had been in the fairies' underground palace, and how much singing and dancing they had done.

When her tale was told, she looked at the posy of primroses still in a vase on the table, and told her daddy that she had learned her lesson. 'Never again will I pick primrose flowers father, because these are a special flower loved by the fairy-people. These precious spring-time blooms must remain in the ground, where the fairies can sing and dance around them on moonlit nights.'

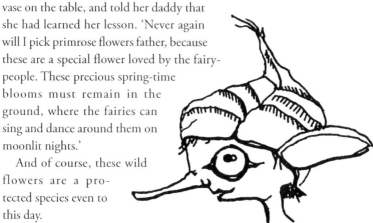

And of course, these wild flowers are a pro-tected species even to this day.

NOTES: The fairy-beliefs and riddles in this lovely English folktale, delight audiences young and old alike. You can make this participatory by asking the listeners to suggest what the farmer must do to silence his farm and home on the night that the fairies invade. Also, asking the audience to guess the answer to these three tricky riddles is a lot of fun.

The rural subject matter of this tale loans itself naturally to many topics for environmental discussion – just make a list of the themes within this story and take your pick: from the decline of the song thrush in the British countryside to protected flowers and species, there are many fascinating eco-topics which can be related to the twists and turns of this classic folktale.

15

JACK AND THE BEANSTALK

(ENGLAND)

Once upon a time, there was a boy called Jack who lived with his mother in a little cottage in the countryside. Sadly, they were very poor. All they had was a cow called Milky-White. She gave them very good milk, until one day the milk dried up.

'Oh no,' said Jack's mum. 'You'll have to take Milky-White to the market Jack, and see how much you can sell her for. The money you get for her will buy us some food and might even be enough to start our own shop.'

Jack put the halter on Milky-White and began the journey to the market place. He hadn't gone far along the road when he met an old man with white hair and a white beard.

'Hello there young Jack. Where are you going with that fine looking cow?' asked the old man.

Jack was puzzled as to how the old fella knew his name, but he remembered his manners and replied politely, 'Good day to you sir. Why, I be taking our milk-cow to sell at the market. Mother and I have no money and there's no food in our house. I didn't even have any breakfast this morning!'

'Well, Jack, she's a nice looking cow, so perhaps I can save you the journey to market and buy her from you right now.' The old man's eyes were twinkling as he reached his hand into his pocket and pulled out five strange looking beans. 'Here you go young sir – what do you say to five beans for your cow? Five MAGIC beans!' He showed them to Jack.

Jack gasped. He'd never seen such strange beans before. 'They must be magic!' he thought to himself. 'Why thank you, kind gentleman. I'm sure they will bring my mother and me much luck. What should I do with the beans?'

'Plant them out in the garden and there your fortune is sure to grow.' The old man winked at Jack as he handed him the beans. He took Milky-White's rope and led her off along the road, whistling a happy tune as he went.

Jack put the beans safely in his pocket and ran all the way back home to show his mother what he'd got for Milky-White.

'My, you were fast,' his mother said as he burst in through the door. 'Did you get much money for our cow? Have you bought us something good for breakfast?'

Jack placed the unusual looking beans on the kitchen table and told his mum about the old man he'd met along the road.

'And these 'ere are magic beans, mum – I reckon I got a right good bargain for old Milky-White!' Jack was grinning from ear to ear, proud of his lucky bargain. But Jack's mother was not happy. She grabbed him by the ear and cuffed him hard. 'You silly boy. You aren't nothing but a fool! Magic beans – how could you be so daft?'

She grabbed the beans and threw them right out of the door into the little garden. They flew through the air and scattered all about the bushes and grass.

'You, lad, will go right to your room and stay there 'til I can bear to look at you again – you, boy, are grounded!' She pulled his ear and spanked his backside as she sent him up the stairs to his bed.

He lay there, sobbing, with a rumbling empty tummy, a throbbing ear and sore bottom.

He must have fallen asleep, because the next thing Jack knew, he was waking up and sunlight was shining all dappled and green into his little bedroom in the attic. He got dressed and went to the window, to see what was creating the strange green glow and the shadows in his room. To his amazement there was a huge beanstalk growing right next to his bedroom. Jack looked up; the stalk disappeared straight through the clouds and into the sky.

'Oh my, it must have grown from one of the magic beans!' Jack declared, scratching his head in wonder. He clambered out onto the huge stalk and began to climb up and up, higher and higher, through the clouds and higher still, until he reached a land above the clouds.

He jumped down from the humungous plant onto a place above the world. Everything was big – very big! He had to fight his way through grass as big as trees and then climb a rocky hill covered in boulders the size of elephants! Finally, he reached an enormous castle at the top of the hill. Jack reached for the doorknocker, but it was too high off the ground for him to touch. Set into the door was a cat-flap, big enough for a lion to get through.

'Wow, a very big cat must live here,' Jack said to himself. He pushed with all his strength at the cat-flap and just managed to squeeze himself through.

Jack found himself in a gigantic hallway with massive pictures all along the walls of the biggest, ugliest ogres he had ever seen! Then he noticed a wonderful smell …

'Mm, food,' Jack said, out loud.

He followed the smells of delicious cooking to a dining room. In the middle of the huge room was a large table covered in tasty things to eat. Jack climbed up the table leg and investigated the breakfast spread. The sausages were as big as whole pigs, the bowl of porridge as big as a swimming pool, the rack of toast bigger than a double-decker bus, and fried eggs the size of flying saucers! Jack didn't know what to eat first.

But before he could take a bite, the ground began to shake, BOOM, BOOM, BOOM. A giant woman came into the room. Jack ran to hide behind the sausages, but he didn't feel safe there, so he dashed to the porridge spoon, but his feet poked out from there, so he hid between the slices of humongous toast.

'Oh, my, look a mouse on the table!' yelled the massive woman. She raised the gigantic fork she had in her hand to spear what she thought was a mouse.

Jack screamed, 'NO! Please don't stab me with your fork. I'm a boy, not a mouse!'

The giantess looked closely at Jack. 'Phew, that's all right then. I like little boys, can't stand mice though.' She picked Jack up by his arm and dangled him in front of her face and smiled at him. 'How cute. I've always wanted a little boy. You can come and live with me.'

But just then, the ground began to shake and tremble and, BOOM, BOOM, BOOM, an even bigger giant man came striding into the room.

The giantess quickly tucked Jack into her apron pocket.

'Fee, Fie, Foe, Fum, I smell the blood of an Englishmun,' the giant sang out, as he sat down at the table, sniffing the air.

'No you can't dear, that's these lovely sausages you're smelling,' the giantess said sweetly to her husband, as she pushed the plate of jumbo sizzlers under his nose.

'Oh yes, sausages, of course dear, how silly of me,' the giant replied and began tucking into his breakfast.

When the giantess went into the kitchen to fetch the teapot for her husband's massive cup of tea, Jack decided to make his escape. He jumped out of her apron pocket, landed on a tea towel, swung down to the floor and began to run as fast as he could. He ran into the hall, past the paintings of giant men and women, and was just about to dive through the cat-flap, when someone, in another room, yelled, 'HELP ME!' Jack poked his head in through the door and saw a big, unhappy hen, sitting on a golden egg.

'Hi, Jack, I'm the hen who lays the golden eggs. Please will you set me free and take me back to earth? My master gave you the magic beans, so that you would come and rescue me from this greedy old giant.'

'Okay,' said Jack, 'but d'you think I could have one of your golden eggs? That would make my mum very happy.'

'Help yourself,' squawked the hen. 'In fact, you could even rescue the golden harp over there. I'm sure my master will give you a great big reward for her – the giant stole her from him too.'

Jack bundled the chicken under one arm, put the egg in his pocket and grabbed the golden harp in the other hand. The harp got such a fright she began to scream.

'Help! Stop! Thief!' she yelled at the top of her voice.

'Ssh', hissed Jack, 'I'm helping you escape from the giant.'

But the harp was too frightened to listen and she just kept yelling, 'Stop, thief, murder!'

The giant heard all the commotion and he came stamping out into the hall,

'Fee, fie, foe fum
I smell the blood of an Englishmun
Fee, fie fo, foy
I smell the blood of an English boy.
Be he live, or be he dead,
I'll shake him hard
and slap his head.'

When he saw Jack wrestling the golden harp and chicken through the cat flap, the giant was furious. He opened the door and came racing after him. BOOM, BOOM, BOOM.

Jack tumbled down the rocky hillside, bashing and scraping himself the whole way, 'Ahh, ouch, bish-bash, bump!'

Then Jack scampered through the grass forest, 'Swish, swoosh, slap dash.'

He grabbed the top of the beanstalk and began to swing his way down as fast as he could. Beans and leaves went flying everywhere.

Down below, Jack's mum came out of the house to look at all the greenery and beans raining down on the roof from the beanstalk.

The golden harp shrieked and screamed the whole way, 'Stop thief, help, murder!'

In her excitement the chicken started laying dozens of golden eggs.

Jack's mum watched in amazement as golden eggs showered down on the garden. Then Jack fell down with a thump on the grass in front of her. The chicken squawked and the harp burst into tears.

'Mum quick, get the axe!' shouted Jack. She fetched the axe from the woodpile and gave it to him. He began to chop at the beanstalk.

The beanstalk swayed from side to side. Jack and his mum looked up. 'What's that big thing coming down?' his mum asked, pointing to a huge shape clinging on to the top.

'It's the giant mum and he eats humans!'

'Right lad, give me that axe and stand clear,' his mother said. She took the axe and chopped with all her strength – and Jack's mum was as strong as an ox; she'd been chopping wood all her life.

'CHOP, CHOP, CHOP,' went the axe.

'WHOA, HELP, WHOO!' cried the giant, as the stalk swung wildly from side to side.

'CHOP, CHOP, CHOP,' went Jack's mum with the axe.

'WHOA, WOO-HOO AHHHHHhhhhhhh …' called the giant as he fell down to earth.

He hit the ground so hard, that he bounced up high and disappeared back into the sky. When the clouds cleared, Jack and his mum could just make him out, sitting up on the edge of his world. The giant shook his fist at Jack and yelled down, 'I'll get you next time boy!'

'Ha, ha, I don't think so,' said Jack, triumphantly.

Jack and his mum cleared up all the mess left from the chopped-up beanstalk – they had enough big green beans to make stews, pies, paté and pickles to last a year. They gave the silly golden harp back to the old man, who let them keep the happy hen that laid the golden eggs. Jack sold the golden eggs at market, and so he and his mother really did get to live comfortably and happily ever after.

NOTES: This classic tale is as popular with audiences today as it ever was. We were particularly influenced by Bobby Norfolk's retelling in Ready-To-Tell-Tales. He includes the connection between the old man who buys the cow and the magic hen and golden harp. He also introduces the nice twist at the end of the story, where the giant doesn't die, but instead bounces right back up to where he came from.

It is a great food-themed story. You can let the audience suggest their favourite foods for breakfast and put them on the giant's breakfast table. You can make this very interactive with climbing the beanstalk actions, fighting your way through the grass and up the mountain, then up the table leg. Use as many fun sound effects as you like during all of the escape and running scenes. The audience may like to join in with the 'Boom, boom, booms,' as the giants approach and they always chime in with, 'Fee, Fi, Fo, Fum' – you can then teach them the second verse.

This story can be told as an introduction to a planting activity – even better, if you are planting beans!

16

MARGARET MCPHERSON'S GARDEN

(SCOTLAND, TRAVELLERS)

Many years ago, on the Isle of Skye, a woman named Margaret McPherson kept the most beautiful garden on the whole island. From January right through until December there were always flowers in bloom. Delicate white snowdrops were followed by regal daffodils, velvet-leaved tulips, wild primroses, lupins and iris, ox-eye daisies, every colour and shape of rose and poppy, glorious hollyhocks, carnations, pansies and orchids – every kind of flower thrived in her garden. And the strange thing was, Margaret barely lifted a finger to help them grow. She pulled up the occasional dandelion and when it was hot, sprinkled a watering can over the marigolds, but that was all she ever needed to do. It was as if the garden managed to magically look after itself!

Folk came from all over the island to peer over the thick hedge of rhododendrons at Margaret's garden. They admired the stunning display of flowers, breathed in the wonderful scents and marvelled at the opulent palate of colours. Sometimes, a sneaky neighbour or brazen tourist would nip in when Margaret was out of sight and help themselves to a cutting or two, but even that didn't spoil the magnificent growth and beauty of her garden.

One year this all changed. And it began with a very peculiar incident. Margaret woke early, as she always did, to the sound of the milkman's horse clip-clopping down the road. When she had dressed and had put her kettle on the stove, she went to the front doorstep to take in the jug of milk, left there by the milkman. Back then this was the way everyone on the island got their milk. He would come round early, after milking at the farm, with the big, old, metal churns on the back of his cart. He would ladle milk straight into the jugs left for him on people's doorsteps. They'd leave the money under the jug, and the milkman would put that in his leather satchel and drive on to the next house.

On this particular morning, Margaret had a nasty surprise. The jug was empty, but the money was gone. Margaret grumbled out loud, 'Well, that's a fine trick to play on me! Take my money and forget to leave my milk. Now what will I put in my tea today?'

I'll be up early to speak to that milkman tomorrow and I'll give him a piece of my mind all right! She thought to herself. She went on with her day, but didn't forget for one second about the missing milk.

The next morning, Margaret woke early and stood at her window, waiting for the milkman's arrival. She had put her empty jug and tuppence out on the step the evening before, just as she always did. As she stood waiting, half-hidden behind the curtain, she heard the sound of the horse's hooves and rumble of the milk-cart coming along the road.

'If he tries to rob me of my money again, I'll catch him red-handed.' Margaret watched as the milkman swung down out of his seat, collected her jug from the step, filled it full to the brim with warm, fresh milk from the churn, placed it back on her step, and put the two-penny piece she had set by the jug into his bag.

'Mm, so you've not robbed me,' muttered Margaret. 'But someone did yesterday, perhaps one of my neighbours. I'll stay and get to the bottom of this, that's for sure.'

Margaret continued to spy, watching the milk jug on the doorstep. Which is how she came to see the most unusual sight she had ever seen in her life. From out of the thick green foliage of the rhododendrons, came a small man and a little woman carrying an even smaller elfin baby. The tiny family walked cautiously up the garden path. They came right up to the doorstep. The wee man took a grass stem from his pocket, bent it over and dipped it into the jug of milk. He then put the other end of the grass-straw into the child's mouth. The babe began to suck up the milk. Margaret watched in amazement as the child's cheeks began to flush with colour. She realised just how pale and sickly the tiny creature had looked, but now that it was drinking the milk, she could see a healthy glow coming back to its little face.

When the fairy family had finished feeding their baby, they hurried back into the hedge, disappearing from sight. Margaret stood up stiffly, contemplating the strange scene. 'Well then, it's the fairy-folk who are stealing my milk. I'm sure I'll think of a way to put a stop to that.'

That evening, before bedtime, Margaret took two big handfuls of salt from a stone jar in the kitchen, and put them into the bottom of her milk jug.

'That will teach the fairy thieves a lesson they won't forget.' She smirked to herself. Then Margaret put the jug out on her doorstep with the tuppence next to it.

Margaret woke up early the next morning and hid behind the curtain, so she could spy out of her window and watch the fairies.

First she heard the milkman's whistle – he blew it to let the village know he was delivering milk – then the clip-clop of his horse's hooves and the rumble of the cartwheels. He jumped down, filled Margaret's jug with milk – he didn't even notice the salt in the bottom – took the tuppence for his bag and went on his way.

Margaret waited silently, watching the doorstep with steely grey eyes. Sure enough, the fairy family appeared from the rhododendron hedge and came quickly up the garden path to the doorstep.

The fairy woman looked tense and worried. The tiny child was very pale and had sad, sunken eyes. The wee man pulled a grass-straw from his pocket, put one end in the milk and the other in his baby's mouth. As the child began to suck, it screamed in horror at the taste and spat out the salty milk. Then the poor little thing was terribly sick, vomiting the vile liquid back up – salt is a poison to the fairy folk; they can't be near it without becoming very ill.

The fairy woman hugged her sick child close as they hurried back into the hedge. The fairy man turned to stare right at Margaret's window, shaking his little fist at her, before disappearing back into the rhododendrons never to be seen again.

'Let that be a lesson to you,' sneered Margaret. 'You won't be stealing my milk again.'

They never did take her milk again, but not one single flower ever grew in Margaret's garden from that day forth. All of the summer roses and ox-eye daisies died within a week. The carnations and marigolds wilted and shrivelled up. No autumn berries or nuts appeared on the trees in late August. No winter snowdrops or spring bluebells showed their pretty flower faces ever again. All that grew from that day on were thistles and nettles. Margaret tried all she could to make it flourish once more. She hired men from the village to weed it and plant new bulbs and seeds. She bought cartloads of manure for them to dig into the soil, to feed the plants, but nothing could bring the wonderful flowers back. Till the day she died, Margaret could not get anything to grow there, except for thorns and thistles. And I'm sure you can all guess why?

If you go to the Isle of Skye, you will find a wild patch of thistles and nettles and thorns near Dunvegan, where Margaret McPherson's garden once grew. No one has ever been able to cultivate this land, because the fairy-folk cursed her garden.

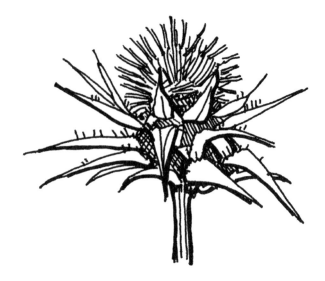

NOTES: *The fairy-race being associated with the growth of plants and natural habitats is a familiar theme from the Celtic tradition and permeates so many of the stories from the British Isles.*

This is a good story to tell when out in a garden, or if your audience are keen gardeners, or about to begin a planting project.

There are many opportunities for listeners to participate in the telling of this tale – let them suggest the flowers which grow in Margaret's garden and which months of the year different plants bloom in.

I ask young listeners why they 'think the flowers stopped growing?' They love to share their answers.

17

THE SLEEPING KING

(WALES)

Once upon a time, a tramp named Tom was sitting next to a dirt road somewhere in Wales, minding his own business, when an old man stopped to talk to him. The old man was well dressed, so Tom listened to him and answered his questions, hoping that he'd get a coin for his trouble.

The old man was curious about the battered walking stick that Tom had with him, wanting to know where Tom had got it. So Tom, still hoping for a coin or two, and actually having nothing else to do, took the old man around to the ancient hazel tree, from which he had cut the stick many moons ago.

The tree was growing next to a well on a small, featureless hill. The old man seemed pleased. 'This is the place,' he said, rubbing his hands together. 'Now give me that stick.'

Tom had told the man where the stick had come from, then he'd gone out of his way to show him the place and he still hadn't been given any coin. He wasn't sure he wanted to part company with his best walking stick and end up with nothing.

The old man must have read his mind, because he took a thick gold coin out of his purse. 'For your troubles,' he said with a smile.

That seemed like fair payment, so Tom handed over his walking stick and pocketed the coin. It had a satisfying weight to it. The old man raised the stick above his head and then brought it down, plunging it into the ground. The whole hill shuddered. The stick sprouted branches, and at the ends of those branches, fresh spring-green leaves. In the ground next to it, a small hole, like the entrance to a cave, opened up.

'That's not something you see every day,' Tom said. He had a knack for stating the obvious. 'Didn't know my stick could do that.' He was beginning to wonder if selling his stick for just one gold coin had really been such a good deal after all.

He knelt down and peered into the dark tunnel. He could see the gleam of a bell just inside the entrance. 'Small hole, that.'

'It is just the size it needs to be,' said the old man, getting down onto his hands and knees. 'I suppose you want to know what is inside this hill.'

Tom shrugged.

'You can follow me in,' the old man continued, 'but make sure you do not ring the bell.'

Tom followed the old man into the tunnel. He was large and the edge of his sleeve did brush against the bell. Tom held his breath as it shivered ever so slightly. But it did not ring.

The tunnel soon widened into a huge cavern, which seemed bigger than the hill. It made Tom's head hurt to think about it. So he stopped.

Burning torches ranged around the wall, lighting the cavern without producing heat or smoke. In the flickering light he could see a circle of men lying on the ground, their elaborate armour gleaming in the darkness. In the centre, raised up on a dais, lay a man in chain mail, wearing a jewel-encrusted crown.

'Are they dead?' whispered Tom.

'No, just sleeping,' said the old man.

'Who is he?' asked Tom.

'He is the Once and Future King. For now he and his men sleep, but when the world needs him, the bell will ring to wake them up. They will ride out of this hill and come to our rescue.' It was only then that Tom noticed the horses sleeping in the shadows at the outer edges of the cavern.

Piles of treasure surrounded the sleeping knights: coins, gemstones, jewellery, pitchers and cups. Seeing the glint in Tom's eye, the old man said, 'You may take what you need, but be careful not to wake the sleeping king and his knights. It is not yet their time.'

Tom happily helped himself to the piles of treasure. But he found that the more he took, the more his need grew, until his pockets were bulging, along with his handkerchief, which he had cleverly fashioned into a little bag.

The old man went about whatever business it was that he had come to do. At length he announced to Tom that it was time to leave and gestured towards the tunnel.

Tom had forgotten how narrow the tunnel was and he had increased his girth considerably with all the gold and jewels he'd grabbed. He tried to slip past the bell but one of his pockets hit it and it began to ring, loudly and insistently. There was an almighty clatter behind him as the knights woke up and sprang to their feet.

'Is it time?' roared the king.

'No. It is not yet time,' shouted the old man. 'Go back to sleep.'

With a great sigh, the banging and clanging stilled, but Tom did not dare to look back into the cavern. He didn't dare wait for the old man either. He started running and didn't stop until night had overtaken him.

He wandered quite far from that hill, until he was sure that no one was going to come after him. He used his treasure to buy a large mansion house. He hired a full household of servants, held many balls, where he served the most expensive wine available and before a year and a day had past, he was all out of money. He took to the roads again, trying in vain to find the place where the sleeping king was buried. Nor did he ever find a walking stick quite as sturdy and fine as the one he had sold to the old man. All he had left to his name was this story that no one believes.

NOTES: The 'Once and Future King' is, of course, the legendary King Arthur. This story speaks of the wealth beneath the soil: the tangible wealth of gold and jewels, but also the wealth of the people who have come before us and the stories they have bequeathed to us. Arthur is a heroic figure, a role model at a time when the world needs heroic leadership. While it might be tempting to sit back and wait for the sleeping king and his knights to awaken and save us, it would be wiser to see this story metaphorically. We each have a sleeping hero inside of us, waiting to be woken.

THE WEB
OF LIFE

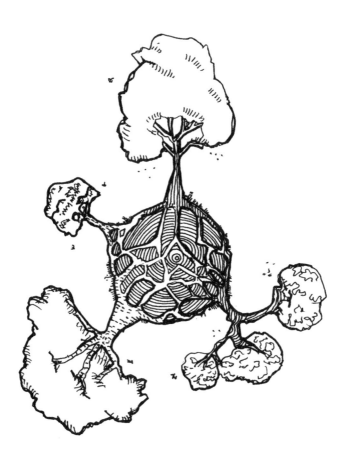

18

THE TREE WITH THREE FRUITS

(WALES)

Once upon a time in Wales, there lived a boy named Baglan. Baglan took care of an old monk whose knees and elbows creaked and who needed help with everyday things, especially on cold, damp days. One chilly morning, the monk asked Baglan to fetch coals from the cooking fire outside to warm their one-room house.

Baglan went outside and looked down at his empty hands. He'd forgotten to bring the pottery fire-pot! Not wanting to return with nothing, he used his wool cloak to grab the coals. When the monk saw Baglan carrying glowing coals in an undamaged cloak, he realised the boy was destined for more important work than serving an old man.

'Baglan,' he said. 'I have a special task for you. Take my crook. It will lead you to a tree that bears three different types of fruit. There you will build a church.'

He held out a long staff with a brass hook on the end. Baglan looked at it. He knew nothing about building a church, but he didn't want to disappoint his master, so he took it. As soon as the crook was in his hand, it began to tug. It pulled him across the room and straight out the door. The old monk hobbled after him, pressing a parcel of bread and cheese under Baglan's elbow and waving him off on his journey.

The crook tugged Baglan down roads. It pulled him over fields, across streams and through woods. It led him for a day and a night, and another day and another night, and then it stopped.

Baglan found himself standing on a hillside in a wood that looked much the same as all the other woods he had walked through. The trees looked like ordinary trees. Not one of them had apples or pears or cherries growing on it. Had the staff stopped working? Baglan shook it. Nothing happened. Baglan tapped it on the ground. Still nothing.

With a sigh, he sat down under the nearest tree and opened his bundle of food. He was tired and hungry, but all he had left was a thin sliver of bread and a mouthful of cheese. Feeling sad because he'd failed his task, Baglan munched absent-mindedly on his food. As he chewed, he watched a family of wild pigs rooting around under the tree, eating the fallen acorns. A crow cawed above his head. Several youngsters called back to her from a nest perched high in the tree's branches. A bee buzzed by, disappearing into a hive set deep in a hole in the trunk. Baglan sprang to his feet, scattering the last crumbs of his food. This oak tree was growing nuts, baby crows and honey. This must be the tree that the old monk had told him about, the tree that bears three kinds of fruit!

There was a flat clearing at the bottom of the hill. It looked perfect for building on. There, Baglan dug a trench for the foundation. Then he collected all the big rocks he could find and began to build the walls. He worked quickly and carefully. Building a church was not so different from building a wall on his father's farm. When it was too dark to work anymore, he walked back up the hill to the large oak tree, curled up in his cloak beneath it and went to sleep.

When he woke the next morning, his heart sank. The walls he had so carefully built had tumbled down and the trench had filled with water. The clearing at the bottom of the hill was not a good place to build. He would have to start again somewhere else.

Baglan headed to the top of the hill, which was bare of trees, it looked perfect for building on. Baglan dug a trench in the thin soil. Then he carried the rocks up the hill and began to build the walls. When it grew too dark for working, he went down to the oak, curled up beneath it and went to sleep.

When he woke the next morning, his stomach growled. He hadn't eaten for two days. His legs wobbled as he climbed up the hill and his heart sank when he reached the top. The edges of the trench had crumbled away and the wind had blown the walls over. The top of the hill was not a good place to build. He would have to start building again, but where?

Baglan thought back to what the old monk had told him. He had said to find the tree that bore three fruit and to build the church there. Baglan looked at the oak tree. There was just enough space between it and its neighbours for a wall.

When the pig family saw him digging a trench around the tree, they joined in, using their snouts to help him clear away the earth. As Baglan began building the walls, something soft bounced off the top of his head. He caught it. It was a piece of bread. He looked up. The crow was sitting on a branch above him. She cawed and a swarm of bees buzzed out of the trunk, flying over Baglan's bread and drizzling honey all over it.

With the pigs helping him roll rocks down the hill and the crows and the bees feeding him, the walls grew quickly under Baglan's hands. That night, he slept inside the half-built church, under the sheltering branches of the oak tree.

When he woke the next morning, he cautiously opened his eyes. His heart lifted to see the walls still standing strong. It took him three days to finish the church and when it was done, it looked a little odd, but Baglan was pleased with his work.

He had left the doorframe empty so the pigs could come and go as they pleased. He'd left the window frame open as well, so the bees and the crows could fly in and out. And the only roof on Baglan's church was the wide, sheltering branches of the old oak tree.

For many hundreds of years, Baglan's church stood on that hillside in Wales, a welcoming place for all God's creatures.

NOTES: Celtic forms of Christianity are known for their respect for nature, as this story demonstrates. This story comes to us from the seventh century CE, when Christianity had only recently arrived in the British Isles and there were very few churches around. Many chapels and churches in Britain were built on pre-existing sacred Celtic sites. This would usually be near a well. People used to visit the wells to drink the water because they believed that the water would cure them of various illnesses, such as asthma, skin problems or kidney stones. When they arrived at the healing well, it was customary to leave an offering to the spirit of the well. The most common offering was a piece of cloth, rag or thread. This was tied in the branches of the nearby trees and bushes. Sometimes the name of a person that needed the cure and their illness was written on the cloth. The rags were called cloots, and the wells and trees were called clootie wells and clootie trees.

During the Middle Ages, after the Protestant Reformation, the Church in Scotland tried to stop people from visiting the holy wells. They said it was superstitious nonsense, but people kept on making their pilgrimages right through the sixteenth, seventeenth and even eighteenth centuries. There are still many clootie trees around Britain, even today.

The wild boar in this story were eventually hunted to extinction in Britain hundreds of years ago. There have been many attempts to reintroduce them since then, including contemporary efforts.

Finally, Baglan's church offers an inspiring model for building in a way that includes the needs of all species, not just humans.

19

THE HEDGEHOG
AND THE FOX

(IRELAND)

The leaves were turning golden in the trees and Fox felt the wind blowing through his fur. He shivered in the woodlands; summer was fading.

'Time to find a tasty snack,' he said to himself and he began to sniff amongst the bracken and the tree roots. A couple of shiny black beetles ran for cover and a field mouse scurried quickly down her hole, as Fox's nose sniffed and snuffled through the undergrowth.

Suddenly, Fox caught the scent of something warm and furry. His eyes followed his nose to a small round creature, which was scuttling across the woodland carpet of twigs and leaves.

'Ah-ha!' exclaimed the hungry fox. 'Just what I was looking for – a warm-blooded, lunch-sized meal.'

Fox arched his back up into the air and pounced down with all four paws onto the odd creature. The surprised animal squealed in fright and curled its body into a tight ball. Fox let out a howl of pain, as his paws felt the sharp prickles on the animal's curved back. Fox jumped sideways and shook his sore paws. He glared at the ball of spikes and complained, 'What did you stick into my paws, you nasty pincushion? Ouch, look my pads are bleeding!' Fox eyed the strange, spiky thing indignantly and began licking his hurt paws.

A small, muffled voice came from within the ball of spines, 'Serves you right, you horrid beast! Why did you jump on my back like that?'

'Well, I'm hungry,' replied the upset fox, 'and you look just the right size for a midday snack. I didn't know you were covered in jaggy prickles.'

'Of course, I'm covered in prickles. Don't you know who I am?' asked the surprised creature.

Fox peered hard at the talking ball and sniffed the air. 'No, never smelled or seen anything like you before. What are you, an armour-plated rabbit, a spikey-coated squirrel?'

The rolled up beast began to shake with laughter. 'Ha-ha, no, I'm not any of those. I'm a hedgehog, you silly old stinker.'

Fox was none-the-wiser. 'But what's a hedge frog?'

The ball of prickles vibrated with giggles. 'The cleverest, fastest, most beautiful animal in the whole woodland,' he declared proudly.

Fox snorted. 'How could a bundle of spikes be the most beautiful animal? I mean just look at me – I am slender, with sleek red fur, and long, strong legs like a dog. In fact, I am by far the fastest animal around. You could never outrun me hedge-pig, you are too small!'

The hedgehog made a low, grumbling sound from within the tight orb of spikes. 'How dare you insult me, you chicken thief. I could beat you in a race any day!'

Fox rolled over onto his back and waggled his paws in the air. He barked a long, hysterical laugh, 'Ha-ha, ho-ho, tee-hee! You are so funny – let me see your legs, pig-hedge – I bet they aren't even half as long and fast as mine.'

'I will let you see my legs stink-fox and I will beat you in a race with them, but first you must promise not to eat me.'

Fox grinned, flashing his sharp, white teeth. 'Okay ground pig, show your face. I promise not to eat you.'

The hedgehog uncurled her soft furry tummy, stretched her pointy black nose forward, and pushed out her strong little paws.

Fox sniffed curiously at the brave little beast in front of him. Then he noticed the hedgehog's stout legs and he collapsed in a fit of giggles.

'Oh my, look at your tiny legs! Ha-ha, your feet are like a mouse's. You only have short, stumpy little things. You could never win a race against me!'

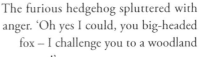

The furious hedgehog spluttered with anger. 'Oh yes I could, you big-headed fox – I challenge you to a woodland race!'

When Fox had stopped howling with laughter and had dried the tears of mirth from his eyes, he finally managed to speak. 'Right, you are on shorty. Let's go – down to the pond, over the hill, around the woods and back to this big ash tree – first one back is the winner.'

'Just a minute fox-face,' replied the hedgehog. 'I don't want to take advantage of a hungry animal, who hasn't had his lunch. You go and find something to eat and have a good rest, to get your strength up. You'll be needing it if you're going to race me, the cleverest, fastest, prettiest animal in the entire woodland. I'll meet you back here before sunset, when you are fed and rested, then we can race fairly.'

The fox yelped and laughed at the confident hedgehog. 'Okay stumpy-legs, but it's you who needs all the help you can get. You don't have any chance of beating me!'

As the determined hedgehog set off into the trees to find some food for lunch and a pile of dry leaves for an afternoon nap, Fox collapsed in a fit of giggles.

At sunset, Fox skulked back across the clearing in the woods to the big old ash tree. He was fed and fresh and ready for the race.

Hedgehog ambled through the clumps of grass and wildflowers and sat on a tree root. 'Are you ready then Fox?'

Fox grinned his pointy-toothed smile. 'Of course I am, foolish hog – ready to prove my speed and prowess amongst all of the animals who live in theses woods.' Fox stretched his paws and legs and got ready to run.

Birds had gathered in the trees, ready for bedtime. The owl looked down at the hedgehog and the fox in amusement. In a hooty voice she said, 'Are you ready runners?'

Each of the two animals nodded and Owl announced, 'On your marks … get set … GO!'

Fox sprang forward onto the path, which led down to the pond. He galloped as fast as his paws would carry him. Hedgehog trotted along behind, chuckling to herself.

Fox sprinted quickly towards the duckweed pond. The long-legged heron looked up from her fishing as he skidded to a stop in front of the water.

'I'll just have a quick drink here,' thought the fox. 'Must stay hydrated when running.' He smiled to himself and sneaked a look over his shoulder to make sure that Hedgehog was well behind him. 'Ha, I can't even see that sad little slowcoach!' He laughed out loud.

'But I'm right here fox!' Hedgehog said, emerging from behind a clump of reeds growing next to the pond. Fox nearly jumped out of his skin when he saw her. Hedgehog continued, 'I've been here for ages, waiting for you to catch up!'

'But how … I mean, how could … goodness me, how did you get here first?' Fox sat down in shock.

'Ah well, I told you I was fast didn't I?' Hedgehog grinned at Fox and began to trot away towards Standing Stone Hill. 'Must crack on Foxy, I've got a race to win!'

The fox jumped up and bounded over the hedgehog, over the clumps of grass and tangled tree roots, towards the steep, grassy slope of the hill.

Hedgehog smiled.

Fox's heart was pounding and his tongue lolled out the side of his mouth as he charged as fast as he could to the top of the hill. When he reached the old standing stone on the hill's summit, he paused, gasping for breath. He turned and peered down the hillside. Surely the hedgehog was down at the bottom of the hill, no way could she have sprinted up the steep slope as fast as he had. He saw no sign of the bundle of prickles and spikes.

'Phew ...' panted Fox, 'at last I'm in the lead.'

'That's what you think!' snorted the hedgehog from the ancient, upright stone. 'I've been sitting here for at least five minutes, admiring the beautiful sunset. Look, isn't it pretty?'

Fox was flabbergasted.

'How on earth did you get here first?' He spluttered.

'Oh, just my natural speed and stamina, young whippersnapper!' Hedgehog laughed.

Fox didn't have time to get his breath back. He staggered onto his paws and tripped and stumbled all the way back down the hill and into the woods. He didn't look over his shoulder, in case he saw the super-speedy hedgehog behind him. Fox was slowing down; he hardly had any energy left. His legs felt like jelly and he was panting so hard, he felt as if his heart would burst.

'Must run … must beat the hedgehog...' was all the silly fox could think about. At last, he saw the clearing with the ash tree in front of him.

'Nearly there.' He gasped for air. 'I can do it...'

Fox tripped over a fallen branch and skidded face-first into the tree. He lay, panting, on the ground, unable to speak, heart beating like a drum. A small black nose and two beady eyes poked out of the ash tree's roots,

'Hi fox, what kept you?' It was a calm and collected hedgehog!

Fox couldn't speak, he just gawped, open-mouthed at the super-sonic, fastest hedgehog in the woodland – on the planet!

Finally Fox managed to stutter, ' You won! You … y'you ... ARE the fastest creature alive!'

Hedgehog smiled and winked at the exhausted fox. 'Yes, that's right. And let that be a lesson to you Fox – never annoy a hedgehog again. You never know how they might beat you next time.'

Eventually, the fox dragged himself away to his den, to recover from the race and his humiliation. When Fox was gone, the hedgehog and all her friends and hedgehog family –sisters, brothers, aunties, uncles and cousins – came out of their hiding places. The hedgehogs enjoyed their celebration well into the night – after all, it wasn't everyday they got to outwit, or outrun a fox!

NOTES: This story works equally well, indoors and outdoors, with prop animals or without props. You can use the natural features of the local area/landscape the story is being told in, as features in the race. The story can even be told as an actual running race with your audience if you are in the right location. Hide toy hedgehogs, or pictures, along the route for the audience to find. You can describe each animal before showing your toy/puppets, or naming the creatures in the story, allowing your audience to guess who they are first. It's a great tale to tell to an audience of mixed age groups.

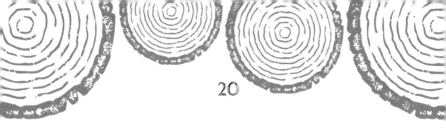

20

THE BEEKEEPER
AND THE HARE

(SCOTLAND)

Once upon a time, there was a young beekeeper who lived in a small, flower-covered, stone cottage on the outskirts of a bonnie wee village. Everyone liked him; he was a kind and generous man. Everyone liked his bees; they kept the trees in fruit, the bushes covered in berries and they helped the vegetables grow on the vine. The honey from the bee-keeper's hives sweetened the villagers' morning tea and the beeswax formed the candles that lit their long winter nights.

Some of the young lasses of the village liked the beekeeper so well, they held onto the hope of one day becoming mistress of that small flower-covered cottage. But when these lasses came to visit, the bee-keeper would send them away with a hunk of honeycomb and a kind word, but a firm word. He was happy living on his own, with his bees, at the edge of the village.

The beekeeper loved his bees. He talked to them, and they listened. If he told them to go and pollinate the apple trees, then off they would fly to the orchard. If he told them to go and pollinate the beans, then off they would fly to that garden. When he cleaned the hive or har-vested the honey, he never used a smoker, nor did he wear a netted hat, and never once did they sting him.

On the day that this particular story begins, the beekeeper was out tending his hives, when he heard a commotion in the field across the road. He looked over just in time to see a large hare bounding towards him, chased by two slavering hounds. He flung open his gate. The hare dashed through and leapt into his arms. He could feel her heartbeat drumming against his own chest. Snarling, the hounds jumped at her heels. In a panic, the beekeeper called to his bees. They swarmed out of their hives and flew buzzing at the hounds. The hounds, stung and terrified, turned tail, running back across the road and disappearing into the distance.

The hare shivered. The beekeeper stroked her long silky brown ears and murmured soothingly. She gazed up at him with piercing blue eyes.

Blue eyes? Hares were not uncommon in those parts and the bee-keeper had seen many before, but never had he seen or even heard of a hare with blue eyes.

He carried her over to his hives. 'Have you ever seen a blue-eyed hare?' he asked the bees.

They buzzed gently around her head. She regarded them placidly.

'I agree,' replied the beekeeper, 'this hare is special.'

The hare wriggled in his arms, so he put her down. She hopped over to the door of his cottage and looked back at him. Laughing, he opened the door for her. She hopped right in and onto the chair next to the table.

'You're hungry, are you?' he asked.

He found her some carrots and lettuce in the pantry, and as it was teatime, he set about preparing his own meal. After dinner, he sat in his favour-ite armchair next to the fireplace and she clambered up onto his lap. She leaned her

head against his chest, her soft ears coming to rest against his cheek.
He sighed with a contentment he'd never felt before.

Some days later, the beekeeper was out in the garden with the hare
tucked under his arm, as had become his habit, when an old woman
came to the gate.

'What can I get you?' he asked, thinking she wanted to purchase
some honey.

'How much for that hare?' she barked, stretching out a twisted,
bony finger.

'The hare is not for sale,' said the beekeeper.

'Nonsense,' said the old woman, 'everything is for sale. It's just a
matter of price.' She pulled a large gold coin out of her purse. 'This is
more money than you'll see in a year,' she said, smiling a twisted smile.
'Hand over that hare and it's yours.'

'As I told you, this hare is not for sale,' said the beekeeper.

The bees, sensing his anger, flew buzzing out of the hive. They
swarmed towards the old woman, forcing her to take one step back
and then another and another.

'That hare belongs to me. Next time I come for her, I'll not be so
generous,' she said, turning on her heel and marching back down the
road as fast as her feet would carry her.

At the market that week, the beekeeper asked the apple farmer and
the bean farmer if they knew anything about the angry old woman.
Neither of them had seen the woman, but from his description they
worried that she might be a witch, someone who uses magic for their
own personal gain. They warned the beekeeper that a witch's powers
would be at their height on Hallowe'en and that he'd better take care.
But Hallowe'en was a long way off and the beekeeper was busy enjoying his new life with his beautiful, blue-eyed hare. He didn't want to
waste his time worrying about the old woman, so he put her out of his
mind, at least for a while.

All too soon, the days began to draw in and the cold winds returned. With the flowers gone, the bees retreated into their hives, using their bodies to keep it warm and conserving their stores of honey. On a cold, bleak, October morning, the beekeeper woke up in a sweat, remembering his friends' warning. Hallowe'en was just a few days away.

At the market that day, he asked his friends what he should do. He'd grown very fond of the hare and the thought of the old woman getting her crooked hands on her filled him with dread.

'If you do not want to lose her, you must take hold of her and not let her go, no matter what happens,' said one.

'No matter what,' agreed the other.

As dusk fell on Hallowe'en, the young beekeeper brought the hare inside the cottage and closed and barred the door. He lit a candle, placed it on the table and sat down in front of it. The hare did what she did every night, she leapt into his lap, laid her head against his chest and gazed up at him with her deep blue eyes. He stroked her long ears and waited as night descended.

The hare began to twitch. He tightened his grip on her. She wriggled and kicked, her eyes wide with some unseen fright. He wrapped his arms around her and held her close.

'She is mine, all mine,' said a disembodied voice, echoing around them. 'I will not let someone else have her. Release her to me or you will both forfeit your lives.' The force of the words blew through his hair, lifting it off his forehead.

The hare became a mad thing in his arms, scratching and struggling. She screamed once, a harsh and eerie sound that cut him to the core.

'She wants to come to me,' coaxed and wheedled the voice. 'Let her go. She wants to return to her old life.' The hare screamed again.

And then another sound, at first so low he couldn't quite hear it. A hum that became a buzz and then grew to an angry roar as his bees poured down the chimney. The swarm circled around the beekeeper and the hare, forming a moving, living wall, sheltering the pair from the unseen forces of the crooked old woman. As the bees swirled around them, the hare began to settle.

The voice growled and moaned with frustration, growing louder and louder until with a bang, the cottage door blew open and the voice was gone. The bees flew out after it.

In the sudden quiet, the hare twitched once more, shimmered in the candlelight and transformed into a beautiful, brown-haired woman with piercing blue eyes.

Needless to say, the young beekeeper married the beautiful young woman, who had been turned into a hare by the witch and freed by the love of the man and his bees. They lived happily ever after, their days sweetened by the honey from their hives.

NOTES: This tale is a popular one at weddings and connects to the tradition of the 'honeymoon'. It was believed that drinking mead, wine made from honey, helped a bride to conceive a child. The story also explores the important role that bees play in pollinating most major human food crops, their presence providing protection from the howling winds of hunger.

21

MOUSE'S TAIL

(ENGLAND)

The cat and the mouse
played in the malt-house:

The cat bit off the mouse's tail.

  'Ouch', said the mouse, 'please give me back my tail.'

  'No, I won't,' said the cat, 'I'll not give you back your tail, till you go to the cow and fetch me some milk.'

First mouse leapt, and then she ran,
Till she came to the cow, and so began –

'Pray cow, do give me some milk so that I may give cat milk and cat will give me back my own tail again.'

  'No,' said the cow. 'I will give you no milk, till you go to the farmer and get me some hay.

First mouse leapt, and then she ran,
Till she came to the farmer, and so began –

'Pray farmer, please give me some hay, that I may give cow hay, that cow will give me milk, so that I can give cat milk and cat will give me back my tail again.'

'No,' said the farmer. 'I will give you no hay, till you go to the butcher and get me some meat.'

First mouse leapt, and then she ran,
Till she came to the butcher, and so began –

'Pray butcher, please give me some meat, that I may give farmer meat, that farmer may give me hay, that I may give cow hay, that cow may give me milk, so that I can give cat milk and cat will give me back my tail again.'

'No,' said the butcher. 'I will give you no meat, till you go to the baker and fetch me some bread.'

First Mouse leapt and then she ran,
Till she came to the baker, and so began –

'Pray baker, please give me some bread, that I may give butcher bread, that butcher may give me meat, that I may give farmer meat, that farmer may give me hay, that I may give cow hay, that cow may give me milk, so that I may give cat milk and cat will give me back my tail again.'

'Yes', said baker, 'I'll give you some bread,
But if you eat my grain, I'll cut off
your head.'

Then baker gave mouse bread, and mouse gave butcher bread, and butcher gave mouse meat, and mouse gave farmer meat, and farmer gave mouse hay, and mouse gave cow hay, and cow gave mouse milk, and mouse gave cat milk, and cat gave mouse back her very own tail again!

NOTES: A story to illustrate the web of life and the interdependency of all species and food-chain connections.

This is an accumulative tale and works well with younger and mixed age-group audiences.

When telling this story, it's fun to encourage the audience to join in with the growing list of acquisitions. You don't have to worry about remembering everything in precise detail, just the running order of characters and what they want mouse to 'fetch' for them – hand the rest over to your audience and they will be delighted to fill in the repeated lines.

If you find it too difficult to remember the rhymes then you can just improvise the lines, as you think the different characters would speak them – accents and funny voices work well. Whichever way you tell it, the audience will have lots of fun joining in, as the chain reaction unfolds before them.

22

THE ELF AND THE SLOP BUCKET

(ENGLAND, IRELAND, SCOTLAND, WALES)

There was once an old couple who lived happily together in their country cottage. They had a lovely flower garden in front of the house, and a vegetable garden at the back. Life was simple. They didn't have running water, but they had a well in the garden that gave them the purest spring water. Every day they filled a bucket from the well and put it in the kitchen next to the back door. If either of them fancied a cup of tea, they filled a jug of water from the bucket and poured it into the kettle on the stove. When they wanted a drink, they dipped their cups in and helped themselves to the cool fresh water. In the evening, the vegetables were washed and peeled – potatoes, carrots, cauliflower, beans and turnips all scrubbed clean in a basin. Then after the meal the water that was left was used to wash the dishes. At the very end of the day the dirty vegetable water was poured back into the bucket. When all this was done you can imagine the state of that water! It was full of dirt and peelings, onion skins, carrot tops, and grease. It was very smelly and very mucky – the old couple called it the 'slops'. Last thing at night, the old man would open the back door and throw the bucket of slops over the garden wall, into the field – one, two, three, whoosh!

One evening, when the old fella was throwing the slops out the door, a small elfin child appeared on the wall right before his eyes. The child called out, 'Oh please don't do that! My mother is so upset. She's down there crying her eyes out at the mess you keep making.'

The old man was surprised. He had never seen an elf before. He didn't know what to say, 'I, errm … sorry … but what do you mean, "the mess I'm making"? What mess?'

The elf child sighed deeply and said, 'Climb onto my feet and I'll show you what happens when you throw your bucket of slops into the field every night.'

The old man looked at the child's feet. They were bigger than his own – in fact they were quite enormous for a little child.

'Climb on,' said the elf. 'Don't be shy. It won't hurt me, I am a supernatural being after all!'

As the old man stepped gently onto the elf-boy's big feet, everything around him changed. Suddenly, he could see an elf-village lying below the garden, under the wall and into the field beyond. Through chinks in the stone-dyke, he could see tiny houses and streets, and little elves going about their everyday lives. But one of the little houses was covered with grease, mud, potato peelings and carrot tops. The elf-boy pointed at it. 'That's my house. Every night you throw your dirty slops all over it. The water pours down our chimney and puts the fire out. My mum is in there crying. It takes her all day to clean the mess away. She said she can't take it any more! That's why I came to show you our world – please, will you stop throwing your mucky water over our house?'

The old man was flabbergasted. He hadn't known that elves lived underneath his garden. He had never stopped to think that throwing out the bucket of dirty water might make a horrible mess of someone else's home.

'I'm so sorry about this,' he said to the elf-boy, 'I had no idea you and your family lived here. My wife and I will find a solution to this problem. I promise.'

'I'll come back tomorrow and see what you have decided,' said the elf-boy and promptly disappeared.

All night long the old man and the old woman stayed up talking. How could they get rid of their dirty water without making things worse for the elves?

By morning they were still up discussing it, but hadn't managed to find a solution to the problem.

The old man fetched a bucket of fresh, clean water from the well – just like he always did. Then he and his wife got on with their daily chores – just like they usually did. They made tea, cooked a pot of porridge, fed the cat and the dog. Then they scrubbed the vegetables clean to make soup for lunch, peeled potatoes and carrots for dinner, and finally at the end of the day, they washed the dirty, greasy dishes. Together the old man and old woman took the bucket to the back door.

The water was very mucky and full of vegetable peelings, tea leaves and grease. The old man pictured the elf village, there beneath the back garden, below their feet.

'There's nothing we can do,' he said, sadly shaking his head. 'We'll just have to throw it further into the field, if we can.'

As he lifted the bucket, 'one, two, three …' the old woman clapped her hands.

'Wait! I have an idea. Why don't we change the doors around?' The old man looked puzzled. 'We'll put the front door at the back of the house and the back door at the front of the house. Then when you take out the slops, you'll be throwing them out the front door instead of the back door!'

The old man lowered the bucket and smiled.

'What a fine idea, my clever wife. With the front door at the back, and the back door at the front, I'll never pour this dirty water on the elves' houses again.'

The elf boy had been listening quietly behind the wall. He made himself visible for a magical moment, smiled and waved to the man and his wife, then he disappeared forever.

The next day the man and his wife hired the local carpenter to change around their doors – the back door was put at the front, and the front door was put at the back of the cottage. Later that evening the old man proudly took the slops bucket out through their new back door. He lifted it up to throw its grubby contents over the wall. 'One, two, three …' but he stopped himself from throwing it, as he realized that the slops would land on the road in front of the house. The elf village would be clean, but all the people walking to town, past their house would get vegetable peelings and grease all over their shoes. Oh dear, that wouldn't do either.

Not knowing where else to put the slops, he dumped the contents of the bucket in the corner of their front garden, behind his wife's rose bush. Then he covered it over with old leaves. He did the same thing every evening for a year. And what do you know? The rose bushes in that corner of the garden grew so well that his wife won all the prizes at the village fair, with her beautiful, healthy flowers.

The old man was happy because he had somewhere to dump the slops. The old woman was happy because her garden had never looked better. And the elves, well they never complained again, so they must have been happy too.

Some people say that this is the story of how the first garden compost heap, was created.

NOTES: A story about staying friendly with your neighbours and about making compromises and compost. In many ways fairies, elves and their kin are the nature spirits of the Celtic lands. In this traditional British fairy tale an elf brings a message that is even more relevant today than it would have been when the story was first told. This story is as popular with older people as it is with younger ones. You can ask your audience what meals they would cook, and what things the couple might put in the slops bucket. With younger children you can count, 'one, two, three ... whoosh!' and mime throwing the water out the door with them.

LIVING IN HARMONY

THE GOAT AND THE STRAWBERRIES

(ENGLAND)

Once there was a young brother and sister, who lived with their granny in a small hut. They were very, very poor. They never had any money for food, or toys, or books, or new clothes. But there was something they were very rich in – GOOD MANNERS! Granny taught the children to be polite to everyone they met, always to say 'please' and 'thank you' and never to be greedy.

'After all,' their granny told them, 'good manners, do not cost anything!'

Everybody loved the children because they were so well behaved and always very polite. People would give them leftovers, like cabbage leaves, a turnip now and then, and maybe even a bone for soup, or stale bread that had been put aside for the birds. The children would always thank people kindly for their generosity and were never greedy or ungrateful for the food scraps.

Each day, the brother and sister would take their goat out along the farm track and hedgerows. The goat had eaten all the grass in granny's garden long ago, so they had to search for fresh grass and wildflowers along the byways. Each evening the goat had just enough milk for one squirt each, which kept them all from starving or becoming ill.

When they took their goat out, they had to run quickly past their neighbour's farm, because he was mean. If this man saw their goat eating near his property, he would run out yelling, 'Get off my land! I own all these hedgerows and the grass verges are mine too!' If they didn't run away quickly enough, he would set his dog on them.

One day, after the dog of the wealthy farmer had chased them far along the country lane, the goat ran right under the fence and into the forbidden woods, the 'Wood of the Little Men'.

Brother and sister called after their pretty white goat, 'You mustn't eat anything in the Woods of the Little Men, without saying please and thank you, and knowing when to stop eating!' They knew that this was a very magical wood. Here the little men lived secretly, and if anyone should steal from their woodland, or be greedy with what they found growing there, then something bad would happen to them.

The goat glanced at the children but she kept right on eating. The children shouted out as politely as they could, 'Excuse us little men. We are very sorry that our goat has strayed into your wood, but the grass is so green and she is a very hungry goat. Please may we have permission to fetch her back?'

The little men were hiding, watching quietly from their secret places. They giggled and watched to see what would happen next. The girl and boy ducked under the fence, and caught their nanny goat. To their surprise, they discovered that it wasn't grass she was eating, but ripe, red strawberries. The goat was munching greedily, sweet juice trickling down her chin.

'Oh no,' moaned the children, 'she is being so greedy, we must be in trouble with the little men!'

The fruity smell filled the air and the youngsters felt their mouths watering and tummies rumbling.

'Dear little men, please may we have a few of your ripe strawberries to eat?' called the sister.

'It's been so long since we tasted sweet strawberries, please just a few?' shouted the brother.

The little men sat and watched as the children each picked and ate a small handful of strawberries.

But then, to the little men's surprise, both children stopped, wiped their mouths clean and called out together, 'Thank you so much for the lovely strawberries. That's enough to be going on with.'

Pulling their goat by the halter, they walked towards the road.

Just as they reached the edge of the strawberry patch, the little girl asked, 'May we take a few strawberries for our granny at home? She would be so grateful for such delicious fruit.'

The children picked just two small handfuls each, enough to fill their pockets and then they thanked the little men once again for their kindness and tasty strawberries.

The little men were very pleased with the children's show of good manners and lack of greed. They were so impressed with such well-behaved children that they decided to give them a bit of 'little men' luck and magic to take home with them.

When the children arrived home with the goat, they ran to the door to give Gran her share of the strawberries, but one flew out of a pocket and landed in the middle of the garden. Immediately the fruit grew thick deep roots, luscious green leaves and the biggest, ripest berries ever seen. The plant began to grow and spread in all directions. By teatime the whole garden was covered in fresh red strawberries. Everyone was delighted with this tasty, new crop. No matter how many the goat ate, there was always enough left for the family for breakfast, lunch and tea. The kindly neighbours were happier than ever to give them their extra cabbages, turnips, bones and bread, because now, they would get a bowl of fresh strawberries in return.

When winter came and snow covered the ground, to everyone's amazement, those blessed strawberry plants kept on growing and producing sweet fruit.

One morning, the mean, rich farmer was passing by the garden and he saw the red berries poking up through the blanket of snow. 'What the devil? They must be my strawberries, stolen from my fields in the summer and hidden here under the snow!' he said.

The children and their granny knew it was a lie. They watched as he marched into their garden and began to gorge himself on the strawberries. He ate every strawberry on every plant. The family didn't worry, they knew a fresh crop would grow back before evening.

'I want more!' roared the greedy man.

'You will find some more in the Wood of the Little Men,' the boy told their mean neighbour.

'But you must remember to be very polite to the little men,' said his sister kindly.

'Say please,' added Gran.

'And thank you,' called the boy.

'Don't forget to stop when you have had enough to be going on with,' the sister shouted after the farmer.

But it was too late. He couldn't hear her, as he was already halfway down the lane, heading towards the magical woodland.

'I own this land too!' declared the wicked man, as he jumped over the fence. 'It's next to my land and no one believes that 'little men' really live here!' He laughed contemptuously as he devoured handful after handful of ripe, red strawberries.

He ate and ate and ate.

He didn't say 'please' or 'thank you' and he certainly didn't stop and say, 'that's enough to be going on with.'

The little men watched from their secret places. They were not at all happy with this rude, greedy behaviour.

The farmer kept on eating all day.

He carried on eating all Monday.

All Tuesday.
All Wednesday.
All Thursday.
All Friday.
All Saturday.

And on Sunday he couldn't stop, because the little men were very angry by this time, and had put a spell on him, so that he couldn't stop eating even if he wanted to!

On Sunday the greedy farmer had grown so huge on juicy strawberries that he looked just like an enormous ripe strawberry himself.

And finally, BOOM! He burst. Exploding into a million tiny pieces.

So that was the end of a very rude man who never said 'please' or 'thank you' or knew when, 'that was enough to be going on with'.

That is what happened to the greedy man who upset the little men of the woods, and some said, 'It served him right!'

NOTES: This tale can be used to help younger children look at issues of sustainability – what happens if we continue to take from the earth without caution and restraint? The lesson of good manners can extend to all our ecological neighbours and our practices.

Where our food comes from and how we source some foods, like strawberries, even when they are out of season, are important global issues, worth discussing.

The spirit of nature personified as supernatural beings pervades the British folk tale. It is no surprise that our children, pure in mind and heart, are the ones who believe in fairies.

24

ST BRIGID
AND THE WOLF

(IRELAND)

Hundreds of years ago, a saint named Brigid built a small hut under a huge oak tree in a place that came to be known as Kildare, in honour of that tree. When she first moved into her home under that oak, it was a quiet, rural place, with a forest and a dandelion meadow and many wild creatures, which Brigid loved dearly. However, word of St Brigid's kindness, generosity and talent for healing spread. Soon many pilgrims were making the journey to Kildare to see her. Some of them came to love Kildare as much as she did and decided to stay. Eventually, a village grew up around Brigid's home. Even the king made a pilgrimage to see her and soon after had a hunting lodge constructed in the forest nearby.

In those days, wolves still roamed the woodlands of Ireland and they were often seen around Kildare. Brigid loved the wolves, just as she loved all the animals of the earth, but the villagers were afraid of them. They were quick to blame wolves when a lamb went missing – and they were often right to do so. Lambs made a tasty meal for a hungry pack of wolves, especially with the king and his hunting parties taking so many deer from the forest.

After a while, the king noticed that the deer were becoming scarcer. He was quick to blame the wolves for taking them – and he was partly right to do so. The wolves had been feeding on the deer in those parts for hundreds of years. They did not know that the deer now belonged to the king. The king wanted them punished. He offered to pay anyone who brought him a dead wolf, one gold coin.

Despite the price he had put on the heads of these wild wolves, the king kept a tame one as his pet. He had been given the wolf as a cub by a hunter who had killed its mother, but couldn't bring himself to kill the pup. The king had worked hard to train the pup and was proud of having a wolf that would walk to his heel.

The king often brought this tame wolf with him when he came to Kildare. Unfortunately, one day the king's wolf got loose. He was an amiable beast, used to living with people, so the first thing he did was seek out the village. A woodcutter spotted him heading towards the houses. Not knowing this was a tame wolf and fearing for the lives of the village children, he set an arrow to his bow and shot the poor creature between its shoulder blades. Then, looking forward to his reward, he dragged the dead wolf all the way through the woods to the king's lodge.

By his markings, the king recognised immediately that the wolf was his own beloved pet. The king's grief quickly turned to anger. He told his guards to seize the woodcutter and throw him in the dungeon. Then he sent for the local carpenter and ordered him to build a gallows, which is when the villagers found out what had happened to their friend, the woodcutter.

They went to Brigid to beg for her help.

Brigid was very sorry to hear of the poor wolf's death and of the imminent death of the woodcutter, who had only been trying to do what he thought best. She borrowed a horse and cart from one of the villagers and set off to see the king. As she steered the cart onto the dark road that led through the woods to the king's lodge, she saw, out of the corner of her eye, a white shadow weaving between the trees. The horse began to shy and stumble, snorting with fear, but Brigid said a few calming words and he settled. The white shadow picked up speed and jumped, landing in Brigid's lap. It was a huge, beautiful white wolf with deep, dark, brown eyes and a long pink tongue, which he used to lick Brigid across her cheek, making her laugh.

They made a strange pair as they approached the king's lodge, sitting side-by-side in the wagon, the tall white wolf towering over the fair-haired, blue-eyed young woman. The king received the pair in his chambers, staring at the wolf greedily. White wolves were as rare back then as they are now, and the king rather fancied owning one.

Brigid asked if the king would pardon the woodcutter. In exchange, the white wolf had offered to take the place of the king's lost pet.

The king didn't need to think twice. Releasing the woodcutter would cost him nothing and having a huge, white wolf walking to his heel would make quite an impression on everyone he met.

Brigid whispered in the wolf's ear that he was to be a good servant to the king and he would be richly rewarded with the best cuts of meat on offer all his long life. The wolf loped willingly to the king's side and laid his head in his lap. The king stroked the great beast's soft ear, a look of wonder suffusing his face.

Brigid took the woodcutter back to the village. As they journeyed along in the cart she told him, 'it is better that two wicked beasts go free than one innocent one gets punished'. While St Brigid was still alive, no wolf was ever killed in that part of Ireland again.

NOTES: St Brigid is one of the most popular saints in Ireland and is comparable to St Francis in terms of her concern for the poor and her love of nature. No collection of eco-stories from the British Isles would be complete without her. Stories of St Brigid often blend with earlier stories of the Celtic goddess Brigid or Bride, who is associated with Imbolc. St Brigid's flower is the dandelion.

This old legend touches on a great many contemporary environmental issues: human encroachment on the habitat of other animals; the problematic interactions that can occur when wild animals become habituated to humans and their food sources; competition between wild carnivores and farmers; the issues of wealthy estates being managed for hunting; and the reintroduction of carnivore species. St Brigid's thoughtfulness and kindness towards both the people and the animals of this story provide a role model to which we can all aspire.

25

THOMAS THE THATCHER

(SCOTLAND, TRAVELLERS)

Thomas the Thatcher was good at his job. When thatching a roof, he knew just the right straw to use. He knew when to cut the straw. He knew how to bundle it and store it, so it would stay fresh until it was needed. And he knew how to lay the straw out on a roof and fix it in place so that it stayed flat and tight, keeping out the rain and the wind.

Thomas lived in a small but beautiful village of tidy wee houses with tidy roofs, every one of which he had thatched himself. Lairds and ladies passing through the village in their carriages admired the houses with their neat little roofs. And soon those carriages were being sent to fetch Thomas to thatch buildings on wealthy estates all over the land. But no matter how busy he got, Thomas made certain his neighbours' roofs were always in good repair.

Which is why they turned a blind eye at first. You see, Thomas' roof was a mess. Stray bits of thatch straggled over the edges. Great gaping holes dotted the middle. And when there was a wind, straw would blow loose and fall onto neighbouring gardens. It wasn't as if he didn't work on his roof. His neighbours saw him up there every fortnight or so, fiddling with the thatch. But it never looked any tidier.

One day, after a particularly windy night, Thomas' neighbour stepped out into his garden, only to find it covered by a layer of thatch. 'Right, that's enough of this,' he said to himself and he marched down to the office of the Justice of the Peace and filed a complaint. In those

days, the Justice of the Peace travelled around the country, so he had
to wait several weeks before Thomas was brought to trial, which was
held in the local pub. By that time, most of the village had joined in
the complaint.

The Justice of the Peace had his footman take the carriage past
Thomas' house on the way into the village and he saw what a mess it
was in. His heart sank.

Everyone in the village was waiting in the pub. They all loved
Thomas; he was a good man and they owed him for years of dry,
snug nights, but they sympathised with Thomas' neighbour. Thomas'
house was an eyesore. A hush fell over the crowd as the Justice of the
Peace entered and Thomas was called in from the back room.

'Thomas,' said the Justice of the Peace,
'except for your own house, this
village could be the most beautiful
in all the land. Your neighbours'
well-dressed roofs are evidence of
your skill at thatching. So why can you
not repair your own roof?'

Thomas looked at the crowd of people
in the pub, all of them his neighbours, all
of them customers at one time or another.
He cleared his throat. 'I have made your
roofs so well that no water ever gets through,
no thatch is ever blown out of place and no
patches ever rot. If I made the thatch on my
own roof that tight, the wee sparrows would
have no space in which to raise their young.
If I kept the edges of my roof even, the house
martins, the swifts and the swallows would
have no protection from the rain. I keep
holes in my roof so that the red squirrels have
somewhere to hide when the cats
and the hawks come after them. If I
kept my roof as tidy as yours, there
would be no birds to sing us awake

in the morning. The bees would have nowhere to make their sweet honey. There would be no squirrels to plant the acorns and hazelnuts in the ground and no one to eat the flies and the beetles that plague our gardens.' Thomas looked a little out of breath. It was the longest speech anyone had ever heard him make.

The Justice of the Peace, whose own estate had benefited many times from Thomas' skilled hands, did not want to see him go to jail. So he asked Thomas' neighbours, which roof they would prefer to have perfectly made: Thomas' or their own. They decided they liked the way things were just fine.

As for the Justice of the Peace, he hired Thomas to rethatch one of his own barns the messy way, so that he could wake to the joyful sound of birdsong each morning and know that the little squirrels he loved so much would have somewhere to hide.

NOTES: In England and Wales, the Justice of the Peace was called the Magistrate. Thatching is done with long straw or reeds, both of which are a renewable building resource. This story resonates with contemporary conservation campaigns to plant wildlife gardens and put up bird and bat boxes.

In some parts of the British Isles, special hollow bricks are put into new buildings to offer nesting places to the swifts that migrate here from Africa each year.

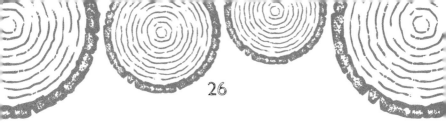

26

ONE TREE HILL

(ENGLAND)

Once upon a time, there was a farmer with a green and prosperous farm. At the heart of his farm stood a low hill and on that hill grew three ancient beech trees, known by everyone for miles around as the Three Ladies. Each spring, when the flowers were just beginning to open to the warming sun, the farmer would pick three posies of primroses, climb the hill and lay the flowers at the feet of these huge trees. No matter what the weather was like, whether it was dry or wet, hot or cold, stormy or calm, come autumn, the farmer would have an abundant crop to harvest.

As happens to all of us, the farmer grew old. As he neared the end of his life, he called his three sons to his bedside. 'Once I am gone, you must carry on the old ways. If you treat this land well, it will treat you well,' he said. 'Above all, you must always remember to honour the Three Ladies who watch over it.'

Soon after, the old man died. To his oldest son, he left three bags of coins, the sprawling farmhouse and barns, the largest field and the hill where the Three Ladies stood. To his second son, he left two bags of coins, the smaller field and a sturdy, stone cottage. All that remained for his youngest son was half a bag of coins and a tiny wooden hut with a yard covered over by hard-packed, stony soil.

The oldest brother grumbled about not getting all of the farm. The second brother complained about only getting the small field and a worker's cottage. The youngest brother whistled happily all the way down the lane, eager to move into his own little hut and get to work on his own little piece of land.

The oldest brother bought himself a wardrobe of fine clothes, a new horse and carriage and treated himself to a trip to London, where he stayed at only the best inns. Before the year was out, he was down to two bags of coins. The second brother hired some labourers to make his stone cottage bigger. By the end of the year, he had used up one of his bags of coins. The youngest brother used one coin to buy a dozen chickens, which he let loose in his yard, and a bag of feed. By year's end he'd earned two coins back by selling his eggs.

When spring arrived the following year, remembering his father's words, the youngest brother got up at dawn, picked three posies of primroses and carried them up to lay at the feet of the Three Ladies. That year, his small garden prospered. The chickens had done their job scratching up and manuring the soil and he was able to plant a small orchard and a vegetable patch.

Neither of his brothers bothered to climb the hill that year. The oldest brother was seen around town in his fine clothes more often than he was seen on the farm. He hired labourers to do the actual work, paid them poorly and rarely bothered to inspect what they'd done. Soon his large field was scraggly and neglected, full of weeds. The second brother's field did not look much better. However, the once barren yard of the youngest brother was thriving and his bag of coins grew larger each market day.

Meanwhile, the oldest brother was down to his last five coins. He began to wonder why his youngest brother was doing so well, when he'd been given so little. The only explanation he could think of was that the youngest must be stealing from him. So he began to watch him.

It was very boring, watching his youngest brother. All he did was chores – chores in the garden, chores in the hut. Work, work, work from dawn to dusk. But then spring arrived and one morning the oldest brother saw the youngest pick some flowers. The youngest then left his little yard and walked right onto the oldest's land. This was it, the oldest thought, now I'll catch him in the act of stealing from me!

Carefully, quietly, he tiptoed after his youngest brother as he went up the hill. The oldest crouched behind some bushes as his brother stopped in front of three big old trees and laid the flowers in front of them. Then he followed his youngest brother back down the hill, across the field and back to his tiny yard, which was overflowing with chickens and trees and vegetable plants.

The oldest brother vaguely remembered his father saying something about those stupid trees, but he couldn't remember what. He did know that his brother had no right to come onto his land and put flowers next to his trees! It was trespassing, that is what it was, and he was going to put an end to it.

The oldest brother took an axe out of his barn. He would chop down the huge beech trees and use the wood to build a fence around his very large field to keep trespassers, like his brother, out.

He marched up to the top of the hill, raised his axe and he chopped, and he chopped, and he chopped at the first tree. A strange breeze rose up around him, but he kept going. He chopped and he chopped and he chopped at the heart of that tree.

The breeze blew into a wind, but he didn't stop. He chopped and he chopped and he chopped through the heart of that tree. Crack! The tree began to fall. A gust picked it up, twisting it around so that it dropped, crashing onto the oldest brother. The cabinetmaker in town used the wood from the tree to build the oldest brother a coffin and that was the end of him.

The second brother moved into the farmhouse. Now he had both the large and the small fields, but by this time barely anything would grow. That autumn, he barely managed to harvest enough to feed himself; he had nothing left to sell. It was only by renting out the cottage that he was able to keep the farm.

The youngest brother, though, he kept a stall at the market every week, even through the winter. The second brother began to wonder what the youngest's secret was. He began to wonder if his brother might be stealing from him. He began to follow his brother around.

It was very boring work, watching his brother. All he did was chores – chores in the yard, chores in the hut, chores at the market. But then one spring day, he saw his brother pick some flowers, cross onto his land, walk up his hill and put those flowers in front of two of his trees!

He vaguely remembered his father saying something about those trees (weren't there meant to be three of them?), but mostly he was angry with his brother for trespassing. It was his land. These were his trees. He looked at the two trees and thought there would be just enough wood to make a fence around the hill, a fence to stop people like his brother from trespassing where they weren't wanted.

He went to his barn and got the biggest axe he could find. He marched back up to the top of the hill, raised his axe and he chopped, chopped, chopped at one of the trees.

A strange breeze rose up around him. He chopped, chopped, chopped at the heart of that tree. The breeze blew into a wind.

He chopped, chopped, chopped through the heart of that tree. With a crack, the trunk broke. The wind twisted around, picked up the tree and dropped it onto the second brother. The cabinetmaker used the wood to build him a coffin and that was the end of him.

The youngest brother moved into the farmhouse, but he never forgot his father and the old ways. He took good care of all of his fields and soon the entire farm was prospering again. Every spring he took a posy of primroses up to the ancient Lady on the hill. After he was married and had sons and daughters of his own, they made a

little procession of it. To this day his descendants still bring a posy of primroses up One Tree Hill and that farm is still the most prosperous in the county.

NOTES: Beech trees are found through most of Europe and are native to the south of England and of Wales. However, they can be found much further north, where they have been planted on farms and estates. They can live up to a 1,000 years and so are the elders of many native ecosystems. While this story can be told at any time of year, it is a nice one to tell around 1 May, when there are primroses about in the woods. Have audience members embody the story by telling it outside and giving volunteers pots of cultivated primroses to put under a local beech tree. Make a ceremony of it. Have fun!

27

THE OLD WOMAN WHO LIVED IN A VINEGAR BOTTLE

(ENGLAND)

Once upon a time, there was an old woman who lived in a vinegar bottle. One day, a fairy was passing by and she heard the old woman talking to herself: 'It's a shame, it really is a terrible shame that I have to live here in a vinegar bottle. I ought to be in a nice little country cottage instead, with a thatched roof and roses growing all about the door.'

So the fairy flew down to the old woman and said, 'Alright then, before you go to bed tonight, turn around three times, shut your eyes, and in the morning you shall see what you shall see.'

And that's what the old woman did. She stood next to her bed in her nightgown and she turned around three times, lay down and shut her eyes. When she woke in the morning she was in a pretty little cottage, with a thatched roof and pink roses growing all around the door. Well, the old woman was very surprised and pleased, but she quite forgot to thank the fairy.

The fairy flew north, she flew south, she went east and west, all about the business she had to do. Then she thought to herself, 'I'll go and see how the old woman is getting on, she must be very happy in her new cottage.'

As the fairy got to the door of the cottage, she heard the old woman inside, talking to herself: 'It's a shame, it really is a terrible shame that I have to live alone here in a tiny cottage, all by myself. No, I should be in a smart townhouse, instead, with lace curtains at my window, a brass door knocker, and a cobbled street outside, busy with neighbours.'

The fairy was quite surprised, but she said, 'Very well, before you go to bed tonight, turn around three times, shut your eyes and in the morning, you shall see, what you shall see.'

So, before the old woman went to bed that night, she turned around three times. Then she lay down, shut her eyes, and in the morning there she was in a nice little house, in the middle of a row of houses, in the town. There were lace curtains at the window and a brass knocker on the door, and outside a cobbled street all bustling with merry folk going about their business.

Well, the old woman was very surprised and very pleased, but she quite forgot to thank the fairy.

The fairy flew north, she flew south, she went east and west, all about the business she had to do. Then presently she thought to herself, 'I'll go and see how the old woman is getting on, surely she must be happy now.'

When she got to the row of little houses, the fairy heard the old woman talking to herself: 'It's a shame, oh, a terrible shame that I have to live here in a busy street with noisy, common people all around me. No, I should be living in a fine country mansion, instead, with a great garden all around and servants to answer the bell.'

Well the fairy was surprised and slightly annoyed, but she said to the old woman, 'Before you go to bed tonight, turn around three times, shut your eyes, and in the morning you shall see what you shall see.'

So, before the old woman climbed into bed that night, she stood next to her bed in her nighty, turned around three times, lay down and closed her eyes. In the morning there she was in a fine big country mansion, with well-kept gardens all around and servants to answer the bell.

The old woman was very surprised and very pleased, and she learned how to talk politely, but she quite forgot to thank the fairy.

And the fairy flew north, she went south, east and west, all about the business she had to do, until after a time she thought to herself, 'I'll go and see how the old woman is getting on. Surely she must be happy now.'

But no sooner had the fairy reached the great window of the drawing room, than she heard the old woman talking to herself, in a very genteel voice: 'It most certainly is a shame. Yes, a very great shame, that I should be living here quite alone, with no polite society around me. No, I should be living as a duchess, in a great mansion, instead. I should have my own coach with footmen running along beside me, and I should wait on the Queen herself, that I ought!'

The fairy was very surprised and very disappointed, but she said, 'Very well. Before you go to bed tonight, turn around three times and in the morning, you shall see what you shall see.'

So, after the maid had dressed the old woman in her embroidered nightgown and bed-cap, she stood next to her large, canopied feather bed, turned around three times, lay down and shut her eyes. In the morning, there she was, a duchess, living in the biggest house yet, with a coach to take her to wait upon the Queen, and footmen and servants to run along beside her.

The old woman was incredibly surprised and more pleased than ever before, BUT she quite forgot to thank the fairy.

The fairy flew north, she went south, east and west, all about the business she had to do, and after a while she thought to herself, 'I wonder how the old woman is getting on, I'd better go and see. Surely she must be happy now she is a duchess?'

But no sooner had she arrived at the window of the great mansion, than she heard the old woman talking to herself, in a very refined accent: 'It is indeed a most terrible shame, that I am merely a duchess, who must wait on the Queen and curtsey to her. Why, I should be a queen myself, living in a grand palace, sitting on a golden throne, with a golden crown upon my head and courtiers to wait upon me.'

Well the fairy was very disappointed and very angry, but she said, 'Very well. Before you go to bed, turn around three times and in the morning, you shall see what you shall see.'

The old woman went to bed that night full of proud thoughts. After her servants had dressed her in her elaborate sleeping attire, she turned regally around three times, lay down on her gold encrusted bed, closed her eyes, and in the morning she was in the Queen's palace, with servants and footmen and dignitaries to wait upon her. In fact there was the former queen herself, bowing and curtseying to the old woman!

And the old woman was surprised beyond belief, and very satisfied with her own royal grandeur, BUT she completely forgot to thank the fairy.

The fairy flew north, she flew south, she went east and west, all about the business she had to do, and after a while she thought to herself, 'I wonder how the old woman is getting on now that she is Queen, I'll go and find out. I'm sure she must finally be very happy, and satisfied being the ruler of the whole country!'

But as the fairy flew up to the windows of the Queen's royal palace, she heard the old woman speaking in the most refined, upper class voice ever heard, 'Why, this is without a doubt, the most terrible shame of all, that we are merely the Queen of this tiny little country. We are very not amused with so lowly a position. Why we should be the ruler of the world, greater than the Pope himself. Yes, indeed, we should rule the universe, and all of Earth's inhabitants!'

The fairy was shocked, and was growing as furious as a fairy can be, but she took a deep breath and said, 'Very well. Before you go to bed, turn around three times and in the morning, you shall see what you shall see.'

That evening the old woman was dressed by her royal attendants in her finest silk night robes, with a silver, diamond-encrusted tiara upon her head. She turned around regally three times, was lifted into bed and shut her royal eyes, and in the morning she was right back inside her vinegar bottle!

NOTES: This classic tale is full of repetitive phrases, which younger children love. Audiences can be encouraged to join in with the bedtime ceremony.

Speaking the old woman's lines with an ever-posher accent is also fun.

The story illustrates the uncontrolled ego's need for more and more resources. It is a good way to open a discussion about sustainable living, with even the youngest learners.

There is a theory that the 'vinegar bottle' in this story, was actually an oast house. These were hop-drying stores, circular in shape with a cone on top – not dissimilar to an old-fashioned, vinegar bottle.

28

JACK AND THE DANCING TREES

(SCOTLAND, TRAVELLERS)

Once upon a time, there was a young man named Jack who worked on the estate of a wealthy laird. Although this laird had lots of money, he held onto it tightly, paying Jack just one penny a week for all his hard work.

For the most part, Jack didn't mind. He lived in a cosy stone cottage with his mum, who was a canny old woman. She knew how to harvest berries from hedgerows to make jams, how to spin fine yarn from the scraps of fleece left behind on bushes, and how to make potent poultices out of the most ordinary plants. Between his penny and the coins his mum gathered selling her jams and yarn and cures, they lived quite comfortably.

But on the day this story took place, which just happened to be the longest day of the year, Jack was sitting watching his laird's sheep and thinking about Jennie. Jennie worked as a maid in the laird's big old mansion house and Jack fancied her. Jennie had just the other day made it clear that she fancied him right back. But it would take a lot more money than Jack could save on a penny a week to make a life for himself and Jennie.

As this problem was going around in his head, there was a commotion of wings flapping and bird voices calling out from the grove of trees that grew on the small hill near the field where he was sitting. Jack had learned the language of the birds from his mum so he listened closely to what they were saying.

'Tonight's the night,' the sparrows were chirping.

'These trees will dance,' agreed the crows.

'With no thought for the feathered folk,' creaked the magpie, fluffing out her feathers.

'It only happens once every hundred years,' trilled the blackbird.

'Dancing trees,' chatted the jackdaw. 'What will they think of next?'

And with that, all the birds took off out of the trees and flew away.

Jack was intrigued. What did his feathered friends mean by dancing trees? He spotted his mum making her way across the field, carrying some bread and cheese for his lunch. He met her and told her what he'd overheard.

She nodded her head wisely. 'I've heard tales that the big old oak tree up there pulls himself out of the ground every hundred years on Midsummer's Eve and goes dancing with the young birch maidens that grow so coyly around him.'

She looked carefully around to make sure no one was there. 'It is also said that the trees keep treasures hidden amongst their roots. But a treasure-seeker has to be careful not to lose himself in the seeking, or he could end up flattened. Here, take a ball of my yarn,' she said with a wink. 'You never know when it might come in handy.'

As she walked back across the field, gathering stray bits of fleece as she went, Jack looked at the ball of yarn. It seemed ordinary enough; what had his mum meant? He shrugged and shoved it in his pocket.

'Jack,' someone called. He turned and there was Jennie hurrying down the path from the mansion house. He waved and went to join her.

'I've come to warn you,' said Jennie, a bit breathlessly. 'The laird's in a right old state, tearing about the place, muttering 'today's the day' and getting crabby with everyone he comes across. You'd better be on your best behaviour today. Better yet, avoid him altogether. I've no idea what's gotten into him.'

'I think I know,' said Jack and he filled her in on all he'd learned.

'Don't do it,' said Jennie.

'Do what?' asked Jack.

'I know what you're thinking and it's too dangerous,' she said. Which was when Jack realised what he was going to do. He was going to stick around till night time to see the trees dance.

Jennie tried to get him to promise to go home as soon as his work was done. 'In the mood he's in, if the laird catches you snooping around his property, you could find yourself fired or worse,' she said. She hurried back to the mansion, not wanting to be caught herself.

As dusk neared, Jack found a clump of bushes to hide behind and settled down to wait. The evening was eerily quiet with the birds all fled, but as the sun sank towards the horizon, the notes of an other-worldly music filled the air.

There was a sigh and a moan, a crack and a groan and the huge oak tree, that some call Old Croovie, shook and rattled and heaved himself out of the ground, his huge ropey roots moving in time to the music.

The lovely white birch trees on the hill began to shiver and shimmy along with him until all twelve had shaken themselves right out of the soil as well. The trees danced down the hill and across the field, pounding the ground as they moved.

Jack was about to follow them, when he saw a dark shadow creeping up the hill towards the holes that the trees had left behind. It looked like the laird.

Jack snuck up the hill to find out what he was up to. He got there just in time to see the laird jump into the huge root hole that the oak tree had left behind. Jack peeked over the edge. The walls of the hole sparkled with gold and jewels, crowns and coins. The laird had a big sack and he was throwing treasures into it as fast as he could.

Jack crept over to the next hole, one left by a birch tree. It was much smaller and shallower and there were fewer things gleaming in the moonlight. He thought about his sweetheart Jennie and how much he wanted to marry her. He thought about his mum and how hard she worked to put food on their table and to keep their house comfortable and warm. Far in the distance, he could hear the strange music and the thumping of the dancing trees. He'd just be down there for a minute or two, plenty of time to get back out before the trees returned. He jumped in.

The hole was deeper than it had seemed and there were more jewels and gold than he'd thought. He plucked a large blue sapphire out of the wall and put it in his pocket for his mum. A sprinkling of soil trickled onto his feet. He found a gold ring the perfect size for Jennie's finger and pried it loose, sending down another cascade of dirt.

Just as he'd put the ring in his pocket, Jennie's head appeared at the edge of the hole. 'Jack,' she called. 'You have to get out, now. The sky is getting lighter and the sound of the trees is growing closer.'

Jack tried to scramble up the side of the root hole, but the loose soil kept coming away under his fingers.

'Quickly,' cried Jennie.

Jack remembered the ball of yarn his mum had given him. He held one end and threw the rest up to Jennie. 'Tie this onto a sturdy bush,' he called. She nodded and disappeared from view. She reappeared. He tugged on the yarn. It seemed strong enough.

Hand, over hand, he pulled himself up out of the roothole. By the time he got out, the trees could be seen across the field, still dancing to the music, but heading back to their hill.

Jack ran over to the big hole. The laird's sack was bulging, but he was still down there cramming more treasure into it. 'Laird,' Jack called to him, tying one end of the yarn to a bush and tossing the ball down into the hole. 'The trees are coming back, you've got to get out of there.' The laird ignored Jack and the yarn, his wide eyes shone darkly as he continued to scrabble for jewels in the dirt.

Jennie tugged on Jack's hand. The trees were dancing up the hill. Jack and Jennie ran as fast as they could down the other side. They didn't stop running until they got to the little stone cottage, where Jack's mum had dinner waiting for them both.

They came back the next day and found the yarn Jack had left tied to the bush. It disappeared under the huge roots of the oak tree. There was no sign of the laird.

Jack did not wait long to put the gold ring on Jennie's finger and soon after that they moved into the little stone cottage. Jack's mum sold the sapphire and bought herself a house on a loch, where she lived happily ever after.

And the wealthy old laird? He was never seen again. The estate was given to his son, who turned out to be a much more generous employer than his father and Jack and Jennie both got a big raise.

NOTES: Jack stories are common across England and Scotland. They have even turned up in French-speaking parts of North America as stories about P'tit Jean. Jack is the working everyman, who tries to live rightly in relation to his employer, his family and the wider world he is a part of. This story makes a good introduction to the complex topic of resource extraction and the concentration of wealth.

Both birch trees and oak trees are native to the British Isles, although oak forests are much more common in England than Scotland. While we did not come across any dancing tree stories from England, we did find some from Germany, the Czech Republic and even the West Coast of America.

Birch trees are often depicted as female in stories and oaks as male. The English oak is the richest tree in terms of biodiversity, supporting

the largest number of other organisms of any tree in Britain. Its acorns
support a number of mammals through the long winter and it provides
habitat for birds and bats. But it is richest in insects, supporting hun-
dreds of species, which in turn feed other animals. Its leaves break down
easily, forming a thick layer of humus, which feeds insects and fungi, so
the soil in which an old oak lives can really be understood as containing
the treasures of the tree.

TELLING STORIES
WITH THE SEASONS

Reconnecting to the seasons, to the natural rhythms of the year, is an essential antidote to the separation from nature that haunts contemporary living. Traditionally, the stories told would change as the year shifted from dark to light and back again. The Celtic year was divided by eight holy days: the two solstices and two equinoxes, as well as four days that fall roughly halfway between these solar events. Storytelling would have featured as part of the celebrations on each of these days. Some of the stories included in this collection are associated with particular seasons and we invite you to mark the passing of the year, by sharing these stories on Celtic holy days:

Winter Solstice (21 December)
St Mungo and the Robin
The Goat and the Strawberries

Imbolc (2 February)
St Brigid and the Wolf

Spring Equinox (21 March)
Maggie's Nest
The Sunken Palace
Thomas the Thatcher

Beltane (1 May)
Stolen by Fairies
The Elf and the Slop Bucket
One Tree Hill

Summer Solstice (21 June)
King and Queen of the Birds
The Laddie Who Herded Hares
Jack and the Dancing Trees

Lughnasagh (31 July)
Saving the Forest
The Blaeberry Girl
Jack and the Beanstalk
Margaret MacPherson's Garden

Autumn Equinox (21 September)
Alder Sprite
The Sleeping King
The Tree with Three Fruits
The Hedgehog and the Fox

Samhain (31 October)
Archie's Besom
Ceridwen's Cauldron
The Tiddy Mun
The Beekeeper and the Hare

NATURAL HISTORY INDEX TO THESE STORIES

FAUNA

Domesticated Animals
Ceridwen's Cauldron
Saving the Forest
The Goat and the Strawberries
Stolen by Fairies
Margaret MacPherson's Garden

Golden Eagle (*Aquila chrysaetos*)
King and Queen of the Birds

Fox (*Vulpes vulpes*)
The Hedgehog and the Fox

Common Glow Worms (Lampyris noctiluca)
Stolen by Fairies

Hares (*Lepus europaeus*)
The Beekeeper and the Hare
The Laddie Who Herded Hares

Hedgehog (*Erinaceus europaeus*)
The Hedgehog and the Fox

Common Lizard (*Zootoca vivipara*)
Stolen by Fairies

Long-tailed tit (*Aegithalos caudatus*)
Magpie's Nest

Magpie (*Pica pica*)
Magpie's Nest

Mouse, Field (*Mus musculus*)
Thomas the Thatcher
The Mouse's Tail

Wren (*Troglodytes troglodytes*)
King and Queen of the Birds

FLORA

Alder (*Alnus glutinosa*)
The Alder Sprite

Apple (*Malus*)
Ceridwen's Cauldron

Beech (*Fagus sylvatica*)
One Tree Hill

Birch (*Betula pubescens*)
Archie's Besom
Jack and the Dancing Trees

Blaeberries (*Vaccinium myrtillus*)
The Blaeberry Girl

Dandelion (*Taraxacum officionale*)
St Brigid and the Wolf
Margaret MacPherson's Garden

Hazel (*Corylus avellana*)
St Mungo and the Robin
The Sleeping King
Ceridwen's Cauldron

Heather (*Calluna vulgaris*)
Archie's Besom

SOURCE NOTES
FOR THE STORIES

We have both been involved in storytelling and environmental education for several years. The core of this collection consists of stories that are part of our own repertoires and that we have used many times in a variety of contexts and with a range of ages. When we began envisioning this project, we started actively seeking other stories from Scotland, Ireland, England and Wales that have an environmental angle. The following section provides source information for these stories. Where possible, we've traced back to an original publication. We have also listed those contemporary published versions that we could find.

The Alder Sprite

Tradition: England, folklore
Original Source: Katharine M. Briggs, *The Fairies in Tradition and Literature* (Routledge, London, 1967)
Also Appears In: Katharine M. Briggs, *A Book of Fairies* (Penguin Books, 1976, 1997), pp.30–31.
Gabrielle Maunder, 'Woodman-Spare that Tree', in *Galaxy: Stories & Writings* (Oxford University Press, 1970)

Archie's Besom

Tradition: Scotland, Travellers
Duncan Williamson says he heard this story from the brother of a crofter,

Neil McCallum, in Argyll, where they worked on dry-stane dykes together, when Duncan was young.

Original Source: Duncan Williamson and Linda Williamson, edited by Linda Williamson, *Fireside Tales of the Traveller Children* (Birlinn, 1983. Reprinted in 2009), pp.65–72

Also Appears in: Donald Braid, *Scottish Traveller Tales: Lives Shaped Through Stories* (University Press of Mississippi, 2002), pp.234–238

The Beekeeper and the Hare

Tradition: Scotland, folklore

Original Source: Sorche Nic Leodhas, *Thistle and Thyme, Tales and Legends from Scotland* (The Bodley Head, London, Sydney, Toronto, 1962. Reprinted 1975), pp.197–208

Also appears in: Susan Milord and Michael Donato, *Tales Alive! Ten Multicultural Folktales with Activities* (Turtleback Books, 2003), pp.81–86

Unknown in *Tell me a Story!* (Andrews & McMeel, Kansas City, 1998): www.uexpress.com/tell-me-a-story/1998/3/29/the-beekeeper-and-the-hare-a

Elaine Lindy, 'The BeeKeeper and the Bewitched Hare', *Stories to Grow By* (2007) www.storiestogrowby.org

The Blaeberry Girl

Tradition: Irish, folklore

Alette learned this version as a member of the Talking Trees Storytelling group at the Royal Botanic Garden Edinburgh.

Original Source: There are many Irish stories in which a leprechaun has a buried pot of gold.

Also Appears in: Ian Edwards, *Tales from the Forest* (Royal Botanic Garden Edinburgh, 2011)

Una Leavy, *Irish Fairy Tales and Legends* (Roberts Rinehart Publishers, 1999)

Maggie Pearson, *The Fox and the Rooster and Other Tales* (Little Tiger: Waukesha, WI, 1997)

Linda Shute, *Clever Tom and the Leprechaun* (Scholastic, 1990)

Joseph Jacobs, *Celtic Fairy Tales: 'The Field of Boliauns'*, (The Bodley Head 1970), pp.21–23

Ceridwen's Cauldron

Tradition: Wales, ancient Celtic

Original Source: Lady Charlotte E. Guest (translated by), *The Mabinogion* (J.M. Dent and Sons Ltd, London, 1906)

Also Appears in: T.W. Rollerston, 'The Tale of Taliesin' in *Celtic Myths and Legends* (Studio Editions, London, 1986. Reprint in 1990), pp.412–414

Helena Paterson, *The Celtic Lunar Zodiac, How to Interpret Your Moon Sign* (Rider, London, Sydney, Auckland, Johannesburg, 1992), pp.31–32

The Elf Boy and the Slop Bucket

Tradition: Scotland/Wales/Ireland, folklore

This is a mixture of various versions Allison had read – the fairy comes in different guises: a child, an old man, and they all complain of dirty neighbours and or the pollution they are causing. In the Godfrey McCulloch version, the elf is complaining about the man's sewage draining into his house!

After Allison had told this tale many times in community gardens, the compost connection was made. Enthusiastic audiences helped to take this natural storytelling step and shape a new ending to an old story.

Original Source: Variant, 'Sir Godfrey McCulloch' in Sir George Douglas, *Scottish Fairy and Folk Tales* (1898, 1977 Edition from EP Publishing limited, East Ardsley, Wakefied, West Yorkshire), pp.112–113

Also Appears in: Variant, 'Sir Godfrey McCulloch' in Katharine M. Briggs, *A Dictionary of British Folktales, Part B Folk Legends* (Routledge, London and New York, 1970), pp.354–355

Elizabeth Shepperd-Jones, *Welsh Legendary Tales* (Thomas Nelson, Edinburgh, 1959), pp.156–158

Amabel Williams-Ellis, *Fairy Tales from the British Isles* (Frederick Warne, New York, 1960), pp.76–81

Margaret Read MacDonald, *Peace Tales, World Folk Tales to Talk About* (Linnet Books, 1992), pp.63–68

Ruth Ratcliff, *Scottish Folktales* (Frederick Muller Limited, London, 1976)

Irish variants also exist, although the authors have not seen these.

The Goat and the Strawberries

Tradition: England, folklore

Original Source: Sent to Ruth L. Tongue, in a letter, Somerset 1917, and given to Katharine M. Briggs, 'That's Enough to go on With' in *A Dictionary of British Folktales, Part A Folk Narratives* (Routledge, London and New York, 1970), pp.505–506

Also Appears in: Margaret Read MacDonald, 'The Strawberries of the Little Men', in *Look Back and See, Twenty Lively Tales for Gentle Tellers* (The H.W. Wilson Company, 1991), pp.95–101

Ruth L. Tongue, 'Forgotten Folktales' – a manuscript sent to Katharine M. Briggs, 1964

The Hedgehog and the Fox

Tradition: Irish/English, folklore

Variations of this tale are known all over the world. Different types of animal racing each other, in the differing versions – the most widely known being Aesop's fable, 'The Hare and the Tortoise'.

Original Source: Katharine M. Briggs, *A Dictionary of British Folktales, Part A Folk Narratives* (Routledge, London and New York, 1970), pp.108–109

Also Appears in: Michael Scott, *Irish Animal Tales* (The Mercier Press, Cork and Dublin, 1989), pp.46–52

Jack and the Beanstalk

Tradition: English

Original Source: Katharine M. Briggs, *A Dictionary of British Folktales, Part A Folk Narratives* (Routledge, London and New York, 1970) versions 1, 11, & C, pp.316–322

Also Appears in: Iona and Peter Opie, *The Classic Fairy Tales* (Oxford University Press, 1974), pp.163–174

Bobby Norfolk's re-telling 'Jack and the Magic Beans' in David Holt and Bill Mooney, *Ready-To-Tell-Tales, Sure Fire Stories from*

America's Favourite Storytellers (August House, Inc, Atlanta, 1994), pp.207–211

Jack and the Dancing Trees

Tradition: Scotland, Travellers

This is a popular story amongst storytellers in Scotland and we've heard many versions of it in many different contexts.

Original Source: Stanley Robertson. 'Battling Don's Tale' in *Exodus to Alford* (Balnain Books, Nairn, Scotland, 1988)

Also Appears in: Ian Edwards, 'Old Croovie' in *Tales from the Forest* (Royal Botanic Garden Edinburgh, 2011)

King and Queen of the Birds

Tradition: British Isles, folklore

This story is well known and told all over the world. In other British versions, after the wrens have won the contest, they never again fly higher than low-lying trees and bushes. This is a good alternative ending if you want your listeners to remember in which habitats to look to find Britain's second smallest bird, the wren. In other cultures the wren is often replaced with the linnet or other small bird.

Original Source: Oral. Possibly a retelling of an Aesop's fable, known as King of the Birds. A version of this story can be found on every continent on earth, except for Antarctica!

Also Appears in: Sir George Douglas, *Scottish Fairy and Folk Tales* (1898, 1977 edition from EP Publishing Ltd, East Ardsley, Wakefield, West Yorkshire), pp. 33–45

Katharine M. Briggs, *A Dictionary of British Folktales, Part A Folk Narratives* (Routledge, London and New York, 1970), pp.117–119

Norah and William Montgomerie, 'The Eagle and the Wren' in *The Folk Tales of Scotland: The Well at the World's End and Other Stories* (Birlinn, 1975, reprint: 2013), pp. 214

The Laddie who Herded Hares

Tradition: Border country between Scotland and England

Alette first heard this story told at a storytelling training day for

Eco-Schools back in 2008, which was the day that she and Allison first met!

Original Source: Winifred Finlay, The Laddie who kept Hares, *Tales from the Borders* (London, Kaye & Ward, 1979), pp.90–100

Also Appears in: James P. Spence, *Scottish Borders Tales* (The History Press, 2015)

Magpie's Nest

Tradition: England, folklore

Allison tells this tale every spring, while the birds are nest-building. She had to make a story-stick to help her remember the sequence of nest – building methods, and the different birds involved.

After learning this tale from Allison, Alette first told it in the Penguin Observation Hut at the Edinburgh zoo. It was freezing cold and audiences didn't want to stay for long, this story was the perfect length.

Original Source: Charles Swainson, *The Folklore and Provincial Names of British Birds* (Kessinger Publishing, 1886), p.80 and 166

Also Appears in: Katharine M. Briggs, *A Dictionary of British Folktales, Part A Folk Narratives* (Routledge, London and New York, 1970), p.123.

Michael J. Caduto, *Earth Tales From Around the World* (Fulcrum Publishing, Golden Colorado, 1997), pp.133–134

Margaret McPherson's Garden

Tradition: Scotland, Traveller Tale

Allison learned this story from Owen Pilgrim, a storyteller who learned it directly from the late master storyteller, Duncan Williamson. It should be noted that Duncan called it 'Maggie McPherson's Garden', but we've given her her Sunday name.

Original Source: Oral – the late Duncan Williamson

Also Appears in: Lindsay S. Pinchbeck, *Stories of the Fairy Folk--A documentary film about three storytellers from Scotland and Ireland* (2008)

Mouse's Tail

Tradition: England and British Isles

This is a very old 'Nursery Tale'. It is part of a large collection of similar

stories and rhymes in which the main character, usually a mouse and
sometimes a fox, loses their tail and has to go on a journey, garnering
favours to win back their tail.

Original Source: James Orchard Halliwell-Phillips, *Popular Rhymes*
and Nursery Tales: a sequel to the Nursery Rhymes of England (John
Russell Smith: London, 1849), pp.33–34

Also Appears in: Katharine M. Briggs, *A Dictionary of British*
Folktales--Part A Folk Narratives (Routledge, London and New
York, 1970, 1991), pp.512

Alida Gersie, *Mouse Wants her Tail Back: Earthtales – Storytelling in*
Times of Change (Green Print, The Merlin Press, 1992), pp.74

The Old Woman Who Lived in a Vinegar Bottle

Tradition: England, folklore

Allison watched Chris Bostock, a master storyteller from Northern
England, tell this to an audience filled with little girls dressed as
fairies, in Cumbria. He encouraged the children to turn around three
times and shut their eyes – even the adults in the audience had fun
twirling giddily around.

Original Source: Katharine M. Briggs, *A Dictionary of British*
Folktales, Part A Folk Narratives (Routledge, London and New
York, 1971), pp.436–439

Also Appears in: Angela Carter, *The Virago Book of Fairy Tales*
(Virago, 1990, 2006), pp.114–117

Michael Floss, *Folk Tales of the British Isles* (Book Club Associates:
London, 1977), pp. 93–97

One Tree Hill

Tradition: England, folklore

Alette first learned this story for a story walk when leading at a Celtic
Festival on the grounds of the lovely, old, wooded estate of Newbattle
Abbey College. Children brought potted primroses to lay in the lap of
an ancient, gracious beech tree growing there.

Original Source: Ruth Tongue, *Forgotten Tales of the English Counties*
(Routledge and Kegan Paul, 1970)

Also Appears in: Katharine M. Briggs, *A Dictionary of British*

Folktales, Part A Folk Narratives (Routledge, London and New York, 1970), pp.439–441

Margaret Read Macdonald, 'Three Green Ladies' in *Earth Care: World Folktales to Talk About* (Linnet Books, North Haven Connecticut, 1999), pp.1–7 (our retelling owes much to this poetic version)

Eric Maddern, 'The Green Ladies of One Tree Hill', in Helen East, Eric Maddern and Alan Marks (eds), *Spirit of the Forest: Tree Tales from Around the World* (Frances Lincoln Children's Books, London, 2002), pp.22–25

St Brigid and the Wolf

Tradition: Celtic Christian, but with roots in ancient Celtic traditions

Thanks must go to storyteller Joshua Bryant for asking Aletter one evening, after a Café Voices session in Edinburgh, if she knew any stories where the wolf was not the villain. This story was the gift at the end Alette's quest for a European story about a good wolf. It is St Brigid, as usual, who offers us another way of being and acting in the world.

Original Source: Abbie Farwell Brown, 'Saint Bridget and the King's Wolf' in *The Book of Saints and Friendly Beasts* (Houghton, Mifflin and Company, 1900), which can be found on the Baldwin Children's Literature Project: www.mainlesson.com

Also Appears in: Amy Steedman, 'Saint Bridget and the King's Wolf', *Our Island Saints* (T.C. & E.C. Jack Ltd, 1912), which can be found at www.heritage-history.com

St Mungo and the Robin

Tradition: Scotland, Celtic Christian, but it has Irish roots

Alette first heard this story while on a cycling trip around the Kingdom of Fife with storyteller Andy Hunter, who ran a small company called 'Story Bikes', until his untimely death in 2015. Andy was a strong advocate for nature and the environment, leading many a story-lover on bicycle trips, long and short, treating them to a feast of local stories and legends along the way.

Original Source: *The Book of Saints and Friendly Beasts* by Abbie
    Farwell Brown (Houghton Mifflin: Boston, 1900)

Also Appears in: Charles Kingsley, 'St Columba' in *The Hermits* (J.P.
    Lippincott & Co., Philadelphia, 1869), pp.286–287

Courtney Davis and Elaine Gill, *The Book of Celtic Saints* (Blandford
    Press, 1995), p.76.

David Campbell, *Out of the Mouth of the Morning, Tales of the Celt*
    (Luath Press Ltd, Edinburgh, 2009), pp.71–72

Saving the Forest

Tradition: Scotland, ancient Celtic

*This is one of the first stories Alette ever told at the Royal Botanic Garden
    Edinburgh. The retelling here owes much to Judy Hamilton's version.*

Original Source: Lord Archibald Campbell, 'The Norse King's
    Daughter' in *Waifs and Strays of the Celtic Tradition* (Argyllshire
    Series, 1891)

Also Appears in: Judy Hamilton, 'The Saving of the Forest' in
    Scottish Myths and Legends, (Geddes and Grosset, New Lanark,
    2003), pp.56–59 (the version included here is most influenced by
    this particular telling)

Fitzroy MacLean, 'The Norse King's Daughter' in *West Highland
    Tales* (Birlinn, 1985, 2005), pp.61–62

This story also appears in the School of Scottish Studies Archives as
    'Dubh A'Ghiubhais', recorded from Miss A. Munro, Laide, Ross-
    Shire by C.I. MacLean, 15 September 1955, SA 1955/164/B7

Seal Island

Tradition: Scotland, Travellers

*When Allison met Duncan Williamson, he told her that the 'seal stories'
    were very special. He passed the stories on from the crofters, fishermen,
    Travellers, and characters he met during his remarkable life. His stories
    are a precious gift, which we hope you will enjoy and also pass on. All
    of Duncan's collections of stories are well worth reading and sharing.*

Original Source: Duncan Williamson, 'The Fisherman and
    His Sons' in *The Broonie Silkies and Fairies, Travellers' Tales*
    (Canongate, 1985), pp.109–117

Also Appears in: Duncan Williamson, 'The Fisherman and his
  Sons', *Tales of the Seal People, Scottish Folktales* (Interlink, 1992,
  2005), pp.127–134

Michael J. Caduto, 'The Silkies and the Fisherman's Sons', *Earth Tales
  from Around the World* (Fulcrum Publishing, Golden Colorado,
  1997), pp.163–167

The Selkie Bride

Tradition: Scotland, folklore

*There are many variants of the selkie story, but this one from Ayrshire is
  unique. In most stories the selkie wife does not come back, but this one
  does.*

Original Source: Anna Blair, 'Seal Bride', *Tales of Ayrshire* (Shepherd-
  Walwyn, 1993), pp.31–35

Additional Sources: Judy Hamilton, 'The Crofter and the Seal
  Woman' in *Scottish Myths and Legends* (Geddes and Grosset, New
  Lanark, 2003), pp.26–29

Donald MacDougall, 'Maccodrum's Seal Wife' in A.J. Bruford and
  D.A. Macdonald (eds) *Scottish Traditional Tales* (Birlinn, 1994,
  2007), pp.365–367

The Sleeping King

Tradition: Wales, Arthurian legend

*The story of the sleeping king or hero is a very common one from Asia,
  through the Middle East and into Europe and the British Isles.
  The story of King Arthur sleeping under a hill with all his knights
  is perhaps currently the most well-known version of this tale. Our
  version owes much to the lovely retelling by the gifted storyteller Hugh
  Lupton, which you can listen to online.*

Original Source:

W. Jenkyn Thomas, 'Arthur in the Cave', *The Welsh Fairy Book* (New
  York: F.A. Stokes, 1908)

Also Appears in: Hugh Lupton, 'The Sleeping King', The Story
  Museum, www.storymuseum.org.uk

Stolen by Fairies

Tradition: England, folklore

Original Source: Katharine M. Briggs, 'The Stanhope Fairies' in
A Dictionary of British Folktales, Part B Folk Legends (Routledge,
London and New York, 1970), p.357

Also Appears in: Sybil Marshall, 'The Weardale Fairies' in *English
Folktales* (Phoenix Giant, 1981,1996), pp. 42–48

The Sunken Palace

Tradition: Irish, folklore

*Legends about sunken palaces can be found along coastal communities
worldwide, because they will have been subjected to flooding over the
centuries. There are versions of this story all over the British Isles, we
chose a lovely Irish one for our collection.*

Original Source: Thomas Crofton Croker, *Fairy Legends and
Traditions of the South of Ireland*, Volumes 1–3 (J. Murray,
Publisher, 1828)

Also Appears in: Marion Lochhead, 'The Sunken Palace: King Corc
and Fior Usga' in The Battle of the Birds and Other Celtic Tales
(The Mercat Press, Edinburgh, 1981), pp.82–83

Thomas the Thatcher

Tradition: Scotland, Travellers

*When Alette first heard Linda Williamson tell this story during one of the
Scottish International Storytelling Festivals, she knew it was one that
she wanted to add to her repertoire for environmental education. This
is another story from the late great storyteller, Duncan Williamson.*

Original Source: Duncan Williamson, *The Coming of the Unicorn:
Scottish Folk Tales for Children* (edited by Linda Williamson),
(Floris Books, Edinburgh, 2012), pp. 94–97

The Tiddy Mun

Tradition: England, folklore

Original Source: M.C. Balfour, *Legends of the Cars* (in Folklore 2,
No.2, June 1891), pp.149–56

Also Appears in: Katharine M. Briggs, *A Dictionary of British Folktales, Part B Folk Legends* (Routledge, London and New York, 1970), pp.377–78

Margaret Read Macdonald, *Earth Care: World Folktales to Talk About* (Linnet Books, North Haven Connecticut, 1999), pp.35–42

The Tree with Three Fruits

Tradition: Wales, Celtic Christian

This intriguing sixth-century Welsh legend has become a common story in Alette's repertoire because of its allusions to the ecosystemic functions of trees and its example of building in a way that accommodates more than just people.

Original Source: Gwyn Jones, *Welsh Legends and Folk Tales* (Oxford University Press, 1955)

Also Appears in: Eric Maddern, 'The Tree With Three Fruits' in Helen East, Eric Maddern and Alan Marks (eds), *Spirit of the Forest: Tree Tales from Around the World* (Frances Lincoln Children's Books: London, 2002), pp. 28–30 (our version owes much to Eric Maddern's fine recounting)

FURTHER READING

BOOKS ON STORYTELLING

Baldwin, Christina, *Storycatcher: Making Sense of Our Lives through the Power and Practice of Story* (New World Library, 2007) – a paradigm for sharing stories in community for individual, community and planetary healing

Felce, Josie, *Storytelling for Life: Why Stories Matter and Ways of Telling Them* (Floris Books, 2012) – a quite personal guide to storytelling

Gersie, Alida, Anthony Nanson and Edward Schieffelin (eds), *Storytelling for a Greener World: Environment, Community and Story-based Learning* (Hawthorn Press, 2014) – a collection of essays from a number of British storytellers who use storytelling in environmental education

Ramsden, Ashley and Sue Hollingsworth, *The Storyteller's Way: Sourcebook for Inspired Storytelling* (Hawthorn Press, 2013) – a comprehensive introduction to the art of storytelling by two teachers at the International School of Storytelling in Forest Row in East Sussex, England

COLLECTIONS OF TRADITIONAL TALES WITH ENVIRONMENTAL SENSIBILITIES FROM OTHER CULTURES

Bruchac, Joseph, *Native American Animal Stories* (Fulcrum Publishing: Golden, Colorado, 1992)

Caduto, Michael J., *Earth Tales from Around the World* (Fulcrum Publishing: Golden, Colorado, 1997)

Caduto, Michael J. and Joseph Bruchac, *Keepers of the Earth: Native American Stories and Environmental Activities for Children* (Fulcrum Publishing: Golden, Colorado, 1988)

Caduto, Michael J. and Joseph Bruchac, *Keepers of the Animals: Native American Stories and Wildlife Activities for Children* (Fulcrum Publishing: Golden, Colorado, 1991)

Caduto, Michael J. and Joseph Bruchac, *Keepers of Life: Discovering Plants Through Native American Stories and Earth Activities for Children* (Fulcrum Publishing: Golden, Colorado, 1994)

Caduto, Michael J. and Joseph Bruchac, *Keepers of the Light: Native American Stories and Nocturnal Activities for Children* (Fulcrum Publishing: Golden, Colorado 1994)

Caldecott, Moyra, *Myths of the Sacred Tree* (Destiny Books: Rochester, Vermont, 1993)

East, Helen, Eric Maddern and Alan Marks, *Spirit of the Forest: Tree Tales from Around the World* (Frances Lincoln Children's Books: London, 2002)

Edwards, Ian *Tales from the Forest* (Royal Botanic Garden Edinburgh, 2011) – a collection of traditional stories that focus on animals or trees

Read MacDonald, Margaret, *Earth Care: World Folktales to Talk About* (Linnet Books: North Haven Connecticut, 1999)

Strauss, Kevin, *Tales with Tails: Storytelling the Wonders of the Natural World* (Libraries Unlimited, Westport, Connecticut, London, 2006)

The Scottish Storytelling Centre is delighted to be associated with the *Folk Tales* series developed by The History Press. Its talented storytellers continue the Scottish tradition, revealing the regional riches of Scotland in these volumes. These include the different environments, languages and cultures encompassed in our big wee country. The Scottish Storytelling Centre provides a base and communications point for the national storytelling network, along with national networks for Traditional Music and Song and Traditions of Dance, all under the umbrella of TRACS (Traditional Arts and Culture Scotland). See www.scottishstorytellingcentre.co.uk for further information. The Traditional Arts community of Scotland is also delighted to be working with all the nations and regions of Great Britain and Ireland through the *Folk Tales* series.

Donald Smith
Director, Tracs
Traditional Arts and Culture Scotland

If you enjoyed this book, you may also be interested in…